T0193584

Getting to the Bottom of ToP™

Foundations of the Methodologies
of the Technology of Participation

WAYNE AND JO NELSON

a force for positive social change

The Canadian Institute of Cultural Affairs

GETTING TO THE BOTTOM OF TOP: FOUNDATIONS OF THE METHODOLOGIES OF THE TECHNOLOGY OF PARTICIPATION

iUniverse books may be ordered through booksellers or by contacting:

iUniverse
1663 Liberty Drive
Bloomington, IN 47403
www.iuniverse.com
1-800-Authors (1-800-288-4677)

Because of the dynamic nature of the Internet, any web addresses or links contained in this book may have changed since publication and may no longer be valid. The views expressed in this work are solely those of the author and do not necessarily reflect the views of the publisher, and the publisher hereby disclaims any responsibility for them.

Any people depicted in stock imagery provided by Thinkstock are models, and such images are being used for illustrative purposes only. Certain stock imagery © Thinkstock.

ISBN: 978-1-5320-3368-1 (sc)
ISBN: 978-1-5320-3369-8 (e)

Print information available on the last page.

iUniverse rev. date: 12/06/2017

ICA
C A N A D A
a force for positive social change

Contents

Section 1: Theory and Background of the Technology of Participation (ToP)

Section 2: Core ToP Applications
Design patterns and variants for each core application and how they apply the phenomenological method

Section 3: ToP Facilitation Design

The process of designing a complex ToP facilitation approach, and a practical process for applying ToP in responding to client needs

Section 4: Study Methodologies

The two core study methodologies for study and deep learning

Appendix

Acknowledgements

Hundreds of people have been involved in the development of ToP methods over the past 50 years, far too many to name. Their contribution, whether through academic research or applying the methods, reflecting and refining them, has been invaluable.

Many colleagues also supported Wayne's research into the early origins of ICA methods, helped him clarify philosophical perspectives, and edited very early versions of the book.

Our colleagues at ICA Associates, Inc., Duncan Holmes, Jeanette Stanfield, John Miller, Bill Staples, Christine Wong, Darlene Fisher and Jerry Mings contributed editing and support through the long process of book research and creation.

Ronnie Seagren provided incisive final editing. And Ilona Staples designed the cover and layout.

Thank you to everyone for all you have contributed to the enduring legacy of profound and useful methods.

Foreword

Wayne Nelson began writing "Getting to the Bottom of ToP" on behalf of the Institute of Cultural Affairs in order to capture and communicate the deep wisdom behind what is known as the "Technologies of Participation" so that present and future generations could use and build on the methods with deep understanding and consistent integrity. ToP Methods are a rich body of knowledge, not merely a collection of tools and tips for group facilitators. By connecting the dots between theory and practice ToP Methods will become more widely appreciated. Think of reading this book as an invitation to dialogue.

New generations of practicing group facilitators may not know whose shoulders they stand upon. Many of us in ICAs around the globe shared a concern that the intellectual giants who created ToP Methods were aging and dying. They were involved in ICA when it was a social movement from the 1960s through the 1980s. Some began earlier through the Ecumenical Institute. Capturing the origins and history of Top Methods was complicated by an early norm of not documenting specific sources or giving specific credit to individuals in favour of attributing the group for the work.

Wayne had to go back to the sources. He spent every spare moment for several years interviewing the remaining "old hands" who were around when ToP Methods were developing. He read and re-read Heidiger, Husserl, Kierkegaard, Bultmann, and other (Phenomenologist and Existentialist) philosophers to disentangle their influential concepts and insights and translate them into language that might be accessible to today's reader. That was the hardest part of the book.

In January 2014 Wayne completed the chapters on phenomenology in a form that I could understand for the first time. Then, sadly, he died of a sudden heart attack. Practically speaking, the book project was stalled. Ironically, another intellectual giant was lost. And personally, our lifetime together came to an end.

The rest of the book, the practical application section, existed mostly in outline form. Luckily my strength has always been on the practical applications and teaching about how and why facilitating participatory processes using ToP Methods works. I decided to complete the rest of the book on what I know best. Therefore "Getting to the Bottom of ToP" became a serial collaboration. It includes sections from Wayne and myself, and articles written by Brian Stanfield too. Brian was a wise and inspiring colleague of ours at ICA Canada who wrote three books on ToP methods and practices through the 1990s. I hope you discern and enjoy the differences in writing style throughout the chapters.

You don't have to read this book in linear order after the introduction. It starts with the heavy work of identifying the intellectual and philosophical foundations and then explores their application in increasing detail. Just for fun I'd like to recommend that you "chart" the book using the method described in Chapter 7, to get a picture of the flow, and then choose where you'd like to enter the dialogue. Let the dialogue begin!

—Jo Nelson

Introduction

The things that we describe so carefully are called phenomena....The word phenomenon has a special meaning to phenomenologists: it denotes any ordinary thing or object or event as it presents itself to my experience, rather than as it may or may not be in reality.

—Sarah Bakewell, *At the Existentialist Café*[1]

Why did we write this book?

Across the world many people have taken facilitation courses from the Institute of Cultural Affairs (ICA) and are using the Technology of Participation (ToP) methods in organizations. Many others have participated in facilitated sessions and seen these methods at work to turn their organization around, put them on a fresh footing, develop a new spirit as a team, and form an operating consensus about the future.

People keep asking us questions as they sense there's more behind the methods than they see. They want to understand the underlying integrity that makes them work. They ask:

- What makes these methods effective?
- Where do they come from?
- What is the deeper set of ideas behind them?
- Is the style of the facilitator as important as the method?
- I use these methods, and they don't work as well as I think they should. What do I need to learn?

---

1 Bakewell, 2016 p. 40

- What is the "plus factor" I need to understand and use to get the results I know these methods can deliver?

The answers are long, but the long way is often more scenic. ToP methods of facilitating participation are much more than a neat way to get meetings to go somewhere. *They aim to build off the deep undercurrents of history, deal with some major contradictions of our day, create a new paradigm of participation, and bring about profound transformations in people and society.*

This book intends to address these questions and articulate the underlying patterns that form the integrity of the methods. This understanding will enable practitioners to adapt the methods to a continually changing environment, while staying true to the underlying patterns of thinking that form the "magic" that makes the methods work.

What are ToP methods?

ToP methods are the core tools developed by the Institute of Cultural Affairs over the last 50 years, based on a body of knowledge derived from exploration of the insights from a wide variety of sources from philosophy, theology, sociology and cognitive theory as well as application in action research. These methods are firmly rooted in phenomenology.

Although many tools have been developed from this rich experience, five core methods are presently formally acknowledged by ICA internationally as ToP methods. These are the **focused conversation** method, the **consensus workshop** method, **participatory strategic planning**, **action planning**, and one that's variously called **journey wall/wall of wonder/historical scan** (one method with different names in different countries).

These five methods are extraordinary in their ability to respectfully guide groups through clear thinking to create results in a short period of time. They have the potential to transform the way people work together in groups.

This introduction explores the broad context of the development of ToP methods and their larger impact.

Section 1 of this book is about the theory and background of ToP practice.

Chapter 1 explores the roots of ToP participatory methods: the understanding of phenomenology as the "study of that which appears to us," as people grasp meaning through reflection on their actual life experience. Chapter 2 describes the formation of ToP methodology through the application of phenomenology.

Chapter 3 explains how the phenomenological method is applied to ToP methods, and Chapter 4 thoroughly introduces the five core methods.

Section 2, which covers chapters 5 through 8, provides an in-depth explanation of each of the five core methods, including the "state-of-the-art" steps of each method, common adaptations, and the consequences of changes.

Section 3, in Chapter 9, investigates the design aspects of applying the phenomenological method in the structure of facilitated events.

Section 4, in chapters 10 and 11, examines two additional ToP methods for depth study. Finally, the conclusion summarizes the book and takes us into the future.

Four stories: How are ToP methods used?

A focused conversation

A colleague was asked to facilitate a conversation to resolve a dispute between two companies, in a last ditch attempt to reconcile before legal action. First he asked each person in the room for the facts about the situation to get all the viewpoints heard. Then he asked which part of the situation upset each person, what bothered them the least, and what past experiences were triggered. Next he asked them to explore possible causes and implications of the situation. Only after that did he seek possible solutions and discuss the pros and cons of each. and what values were important to hold in an ultimate solution. Finally, he asked them to draw the possibilities together into a solution that would work for everyone. In just two hours of guided discussion, the two companies had worked out a solution they could both support and saved the time, cost and acrimony of legal action.

A consensus workshop

A city planning department and a developer had been at odds over the details of redeveloping a mall for several years, and decided to try a different approach to come to an agreement on the details. They brought together department people, the developer's organization, and community representatives for a workshop on the values they wanted to hold in the project. Each stakeholder brainstormed the values that were important to them. Then they clustered all of the individual values together to find the larger patterns. When they named each of the clusters, they realized they had a set of common values that they all agreed on. Then they were able to create a model for the redevelopment based on those shared values. The developer, who had been resistant at first, commented, "We should use this process for all our projects."

A strategic planning retreat

A community health centre decided to involve staff and community members with their Board and executive in creating a strategic plan. They started with an historical scan or journey wall of their history, which involved everyone and created a story of success in the midst of sometimes formidable obstacles. The next step was to capture their hopes and dreams for the organization and the community's health in a shared vision. Next, they identified obstacles and the underlying contradictions that were prevented the vision from being realized. They were able to identify, for example, that their incredibly cramped space and the chronic lack of funds was caused by an overreliance on a single funding source.

Then they were able to create strategies to address all the obstacles. One strategy was to involve the board in raising funds from new sources to build a new health centre. Action plans were created for each strategy, and within just five years the new building was underway. Community people became actively involved in the work of the centre as a result of having taken part in the planning.

A long-term change project

Sometimes it takes a while for a client to trust the facilitator to deal with the real issue. In one case, the client was a private school with a specific philosophy. The initial request was for strategic planning with the Board and staff members, which gave everyone a common direction to move in. But even in the initial interviews it was clear that people really wanted to deal with a different topic: "Were they as a school tied to an old understanding of their school's philosophy, or were they moving forward into an understanding that responded to today's realities?" Some people were very attached to a traditional view, and others were trying to move it into a more modern context. Discussions felt like walking on eggshells, and the tension easily ratcheted up. Some foundational work beyond the strategic planning was necessary if the school was going to break through the impasse.

They began the next session with a *gallery walk*, as small groups walked around the room to see flipcharts with different questions that focused on "What is our philosophy and how does it impact the school?" Each group added information to each question. The summary of that work objectified their common understandings and how their disagreements were affecting the school.

Using that information the group engaged in an image change exercise in another gallery walk. This time they asked a new set of questions:

The current reality
- What are the present behaviours that we are not pleased with?
- What is our current image that is responsible for this behaviour?
- What messages keep this image in place?
- What set of values lock this image in place?

The desired future
- What new behaviours could replace the behaviours we're not pleased with?
- What positive qualities do we already have that can help us shift our image?
- What is the image that will generate new behaviours to move toward our new vision?
- What are the values that will hold the new image in place?
- What messages do you need to beam at yourself to hold the image in place?

When they had answered their questions they did a physical exercise to "ground" the old and new images and experience how they were different on the other side of the exercise, ending with a reflective conversation about what it would take to live out of the new image in the midst of the day-to-day stresses of running the school.

The staff realized through this process that they were not really opposed to each other about the direction of the school and the role of their underlying philosophy. The shift in understanding raised questions for some individuals whether they in fact wanted to shift their usual stance and stay at the school or whether it might be better to move elsewhere.

The actual change was noticed two months later at the beginning of the next school year when the whole mood of the school was palpably different. Any hints of dissention around their philosophy had evaporated. They now found themselves able to co-operate in all kinds of new ways.

What was the social context where this discipline developed?

Group process facilitation as we know it today has its origins in Kurt Lewin's work in the 1940s as one of the first to study the social psychology of small group communication. His work with group dynamics, creativity, brainstorming, and action research led to the realization that working in participatory groups led to better decisions, greater commitment and improved results[2]. In their organizational development work, many management consultants cultivated skills in leading groups and experimented with ways of improving group work through participation. It was during this time that many now common approaches, methods and techniques were created, such as nominal group technique.

ICA was heavily influenced by this early work, initially in group study methods and then in using facilitation to elicit participation in community development work in the 1960s and '70s, under the banner of "participatory development."

The term *facilitation* began to surface broadly in the 1980s as what had been one of the skills used by management consultants started to evolve into a profession. Many consultants adopted a facilitative approach and some began placing their focus entirely on facilitation.

After 1984, ICA began to use the term and focus on organizations and companies as facilitation clients. Some ICA offices began to do formal training in using methods to facilitate groups. In 1988 the first annual meeting of facilitators who used ICA methods was held to share experiences and insights. In 1989 ICA published its first book on facilitation, *Winning Through Participation*, and trademarked the process as the Technology of Participation™. In the early 1990s facilitation began to be recognized as a profession, separate from consulting or training. The number of people working full-time as facilitators increased dramatically during the mid '90s and professional firms began to emerge.

The professional organization International Association of Facilitators (IAF) was established in 1994 and several other facilitator and training associations were formed around that time. Both IAF and ICA developed professional standards of competence and evidence-based assessments for professional certification. Thousands of professional facilitators are now practicing in every sector around the world. Participation has become a common tenet of organizational planning, strategy development, implementation and decision-making in organizations as well as the core of public consultation and engagement efforts.

---

2 Rogers, Everett. *A History of Communication Study: A Biological Approach*. New York, The Free Press, 1944.

What can ToP Methods do for a community or organization?

At the simplest level, the ToP **focused conversation** and **consensus workshop** methods help a group to think through their topic clearly and come up with the wisest result. Individuals in the group hear others and feel that they have been heard. Often this changes how they participate, from aggressive pushing of their positions to co-creating solutions together. A frequently heard comment at the end of a workshop is "I'm not alone–there are other people who think like me!"

At a deeper level, the ToP strategic planning process allows a group to appreciatively acknowledge how they are a part of whatever holds them back, and frees them to create useful solutions that they are committed to. This experience can transform a group culture from victimization and paralysis to grounded hope that they can collectively change their situation.

A longer intervention with a group also incorporates thinking through the underlying images that hold their group back, and changing these images through successful action. For example, an image that community initiative is always dependent on outside funding can be changed when a community holds a local workday that costs next to nothing and cleans up the streets and vacant lots, creating a vibrant environment.

How do ToP methods address some major challenges of our time?

The revolutionary force of this century is the awakening of a deep human capacity that is connected with generative social fields. The revolutionary force in our time is the "I-in-we" or "I-in-now" awareness that can help us navigate our journey . . . that can activate generative social fields . . . . It's a power of presence that we can activate and bring into being wherever we are. It operates from the present moment, from the now . . . . Every human being and social system can wake up and cultivate this deeper source of creativity and consciousness. It also helps us to be more practical: The more we develop this source capacity of the I-in-now, the greater our ability to deal with the high-pressure, high-complexity situations, and everyday disruptions we face.

—Otto Scharmer[3]

Promoting a culture of participation

The rest of this introduction is adapted from a paper written by Brian Stanfield, who was an educator and researcher with ICA Canada and the author of *The Courage to Lead* and other books.

Shifts in polity, such as the devolution of federal and provincial powers to the local level, the gradual move from hierarchy to heterarchy and the decentralization of power, and the collapsing pyramids of corporate power are all giving more opportunity for localized participation.

---

3 Scharmer, Otto. *Theory U: Leading from the Future as It Emerges. The Social Technology of Presencing.* San Francisco, Berrett-Koehler Publishers, 2009.

The rise of alternative movements in fields as diverse as economics, social organizations, health, education and religion creates a climate for community-based forms of economics, increasing opportunities for NGOs and non-profits, and do-it-yourself approaches to health care, education, learning and spirituality. These areas provide endless opportunities for participation, whether through personal projects, support groups, policy formulation ventures, local entrepreneurship, learning circles, or community economic development groups.

The time is ripe to promote the way, or culture, of participation. Facilitation skills become a critical tool. This culture will be based on a new philosophy of participation that can be learned indirectly through the methods themselves, or more directly through training. This culture of participation is in tune with the trends of the times, and is aimed at the contradictions.

The ToP methods of facilitation derive from observations of life processes, and, as such, they are universally applicable, as demonstrated by their use over the last 50 years in at least 50 nations, and every major culture. They are based on the fact that life at every moment presents both limits and possibilities; that each individual is unique and unrepeatable; that everyone is responsible; and that the task of life is always to build the future that seems necessary. The methods acknowledge that a human being is body, heart, mind and spirit, and that transformation is possible even in the most impossible situation. Whether these messages come across directly or indirectly, the world needs them.

The ToP methods are based on what can be called a trans-establishment stance. While acknowledging the necessity of both the establishment (the tradition) and disestablishment (loyal opposition) in society, and while participating in either of these dynamics from time to time, those who belong to the trans-establishment don't identify with either one. They operate as if there were no enemies; they see everyone as potential allies in building the future.

Finally, participation through ToP methods can shift the style of organizations. It promotes the way of partnership and cooperation rather than competition. In large organizations, participation shifts people's image from being anonymous cogs in a machine to being creative individuals whose input is valued; it overcomes feelings of meaninglessness and powerlessness. It shifts the images of those in charge from being managers of staff to being leaders of people who provide, not orders and memos, but vision, inspiration, motivation and direction.

Transform social style

The facilitation methods have the potential to change how people talk to each other. Managers, instead of chastising subordinates, can engage them in a conversation that becomes a learning experience for the subordinate as well as the manager. The **focused conversation** method gives people ways to reflect in depth on key experiences in their lives, to drain the depth together from shared experiences rather than merely criticizing; it offers a way to resolve conflicts between people and to deal authentically with issues of value. The process itself is a prime learning tool. The **workshop method** immediately engages a group in pooling its creativity to solve a problem or create a model. Brainstorming and gestalting become the way of funneling creativity. ToP **strategic planning** is not only a form of consultation for an organization. It can become a way for people to think, act and respond to the challenges of life.

Finally, the intent of ICA is to put the tools for participation in the hands of everyone, and enable anyone in any situation to be equipped to put on the mantle of leadership in order to lead a group to a new place, or an organization in a new direction. It is not much of an exaggeration to say that these methods are intended to put consultants out of a job.

Address the sociological contradictions

Many organizations are still riddled with hierarchies, pyramid climbing and status-seeking. The power structure discourages forms of real participation in decision-making. CEOs and mid-level executives distrust participation of front-line workers either because they think workers don't know enough to be able to make good decisions about their situation, or because, if participation empowers them, some execs might lose their jobs.

When people think of the public sector, they tend to equate participation with voting in elections, where their responsibility ends and the government's starts. Others make efforts to participate in shaping public policy but are blocked by a structure that allows only well filtered input but no opportunity to do real planning. Public meetings tend to have experts on stage who make presentations and receive questions 'from the floor' rather than real engagement in thinking through recommendations.

The voluntary sector offers more opportunities for direct participation but is hampered by haphazard ways of operating. They don't always know how to engage and channel the creativity and motivation of their constituents. There is great good will but often a dearth of practical skills.

The local sector also provides many opportunities for engagement in small businesses and neighbourhood groups but is often hampered by the victim image that insists on blaming the government for all its problems. Local citizens' participation is often limited to lobbying their elected representatives. They may not see themselves as having either power or responsibility. The image of being victims of an external structure paralyzes individual motivation and responsibility.

ToP methods comprehensively address these gaps by bringing grounded, respectful participation methods that not only provide a structured means of direct positive contribution, but encourage responsibility for the results.

Build social capital

Social capital is defined by the Oxford dictionary as "the networks of relationships among people who live and work in a particular society, enabling that society to function effectively." It can also be described as the capacity of a group to work together to make a difference in their lives. Social capital is built through trust and experiences of success. In the current overemphasis on individualism and to groups who think very much like we do, social capital is undermined by increased attention to real and imagined threats. Time pressures and distractions such as social media prevent people being exposed to other perspectives and from having in-depth conversations with each other that lead to respect and trust.

ToP methods help build social capital by creating an ambiance where people hear each other, and together build meaning that is beyond each individual's perspective. The methods encourage taking collective as well as individual responsibility for results. They acknowledge the reality of gaps and obstacles while building on the positive to create future directions. They foster common understanding and will, rather than creating a divisive adversarial environment.

And the journey begins

This book encourages you to examine the philosophical roots of the methods and then the methods themselves to explore their usefulness in your own situations. Let's begin the journey.

Section 1

Theory and Background of the Technology of Participation (ToP)

So what exactly is phenomenology? It is essentially a method rather than a set of theories, and—at the risk of wildly oversimplifying—its basic approach can be conveyed through a two-word command: DESCRIBE PHENOMENA.

—Sarah Bakewell, *At the Existentialist Café*[4]

---

4 Bakewell, 2016, p 40

1.
Understanding Phenomenology, the Root of ToP Methodology

The phenomenologists' leading thinker, Edmund Husserl, provided a rallying cry, "To the things themselves!" It meant: don't waste time on the interpretations that accrue upon things, and especially don't waste time wondering if the things are real. Just look at this that's presenting itself to you, whatever this may be, and describe it as precisely as possible."

—Sarah Bakewell, *At the Existentialist Café*[5]

The first two chapters of this book focus directly on the academic roots of the Technology of Participation (ToP™) methods in phenomenology. To really understand the integrity of ToP methods and why they work universally, it is helpful to know the underlying thinking processes that gave birth to them. Chapter 1 digs deeply into what phenomenology is and where it came from, and Chapter 2 expands the application of phenomenology to the development of ToP methods.

Some presuppositions of the phenomenological process

We find the reality of life in the palpable, observable, sensory world. Authentic feelings and emotions derive from this empirical experience—whatever we encounter. The internal data from feelings, emotions and associations is just as real as the externally observable data, and must be considered seriously in making decisions. Meaning is created out of the mundane encounters in the midst of life. It is not something that is found in some mountaintop experience or esoteric literature. Meaning is something that we all have to work at constantly, through processing the actual life we have on our hands. Processing insight about life involves projecting that insight out into the future. As we decide future implications for action, our reflection connects us to the world in ways that are real.

The thinking behind these presuppositions is explored further here.

---

5   Bakewell, 2016, p 2

An overview of phenomenology as a discipline

While phenomenology has roots in the work of Kant, Hegel and Brentano, the discipline as we know it today was first formally announced by Edmund Husserl in his 1901 book *Logical Investigations* and more clearly described in *Ideas Pertaining to a Pure Phenomenology and to a Phenomenological Philosophy* in 1913.

Philosophers key to the development of phenomenology include Martin Heidegger, Max Scheler, Maurice Merleau-Ponty, Jean-Paul Sartre, Paul Ricoeur and a wide variety of others.

The word *phenomenology* combines *phenomenon* and *logos, the study of that which appears to us.* The purpose of phenomenology is to try to grasp the meaning of something through reflection on our actual life experience. Phenomenology examines the full range of human experience. It looks at physical sensations and perception, thought, memory, imagination, emotion, desire, language, will and volition, action, and social activity. It can be used in the formation of understanding, insight and meaning as well as more practical things like problem solving, organizing and planning. The scope of issues, concerns and situations this methodology can address is, therefore, rather vast.

Phenomenology has taken many forms, often described as movements or traditions. Transcendental phenomenology "stands beyond" human experience to observe and describe it. The existential movement is focused on the ontology of lived experience and ways of being in the world. Hermeneutical phenomenology is concerned with meaning and interpretation. Ethical phenomenology focuses on forms of responsibility and vocation as life purpose. When applied to a professional discipline such as psychology, medicine, education, nursing or counseling, it is called a phenomenology of practice[6]. ToP methodology is one of many specific applications that use the insights, approach and methods of phenomenology.

Martin Heidegger describes phenomenology by saying its purpose is to "let that which shows itself be seen from itself in the very way in which it shows itself from itself."[7] This small sentence points to three critical aspects that form the foundations of phenomenology as a discipline: intentional focus, radical openness and methods of inquiry.

Intentional focus

The first foundation is intentional focus, often referred to by phenomenologists as *intentionality*. In this usage, the word intentional means that our consciousness is always directed toward something, whether it is as simple and direct as a traffic light or as ephemeral as an experience, a feeling or a memory. It

---

6 Van Manen, 2007. In fact, van Manen at the University of Alberta founded the journal *Phenomenology & Practice* dedicated to its practice, for which he set the context in an extended article in the first issue.

7 Heidegger, 1962, p. 58

may be a concern, a question or an idea, but consciousness is always focused on something.

All human experience is grounded in "care". We show up in the world and we just care—our consciousness is always focused on something, the things that are important to us. It is not that we *should* care. There is no particular imperative to care, we just do. Care is an indicative, or something that just exists—the most foundational dimension of what it means to be human. To be is to care. To live is to have concerns about our life, our family, our work and our world. These everyday cares are not simply what we must live with, but they are the very places we find meaning and purpose in our lives. It is within the multitude of real cares in this world that each of us discovers what it means to be human.

That care can be described, because it always appears as care *about* something tangible in our situation. Rudolph Bultmann describes our normal care in stages ranging from the most basic care for sustenance to our sense of duty and purpose.[8] He says we are driven into life by these cares and life itself leaves them finally unfulfilled. Yet they remain, and we find ourselves still focused on our concerns—the things we care about. They may be internal, like the quality of our character or ways to resolve a personal issue. They may be external, such as a concern about water quality or a way to make a project more successful.

"The thing itself," the specific concern, is the ground and focus of an inquiry. Our attention and consciousness are brought to bear on a very real something we are concerned about, something that exists within a socio-historical context. If an inquiry is to reveal something of significance, it begins with a concrete, real aspect of our experience. We seek to gather what information we can about it as it is and our experience of it.

For example, if we are concerned about the quality of our meetings, a group might reflect on the experience of a difficult meeting, a so-so meeting, a great meeting and, most helpfully, all varieties of our experience. We describe those real experiences and "ground" our conversations in lived reality. Those specific experiences become our reference points for further examination of what could improve our meetings and for choices about how we will conduct future meetings.

Radical openness

The second critical aspect of phenomenology as a discipline is radical openness, in which we let the focus of our inquiry "speak for itself in its own way." We examine the focus of our inquiry as it is without assumptions, presuppositions or expectations. We stand aside and examine conventional wisdom, allowing us to see life as it is. This "putting brackets or parentheses around" all understandings of truth so the object of our inquiry can be described and examined on its own merits is one of the core aspects of phenomenological inquiry. We make a separation between our thoughts and our thinking. That is to say, we step aside from our thoughts so we can examine them in their appropriate context.

---

8 Johnson, 1991, p. 243

For example, when inquiring about a chair, we stand aside from our assumptions about what constitutes an ideal chair, including the common assumptions about construction, comfort, materials and style, so we can focus on the chairs we experience. The same principle applies to our more important inquiries about ourselves and the world around us. In inquiry we stand aside from various aspects of our life in order to observe, examine and make new choices.

When we are involved in an inquiry, assumptions, judgments, theories, presuppositions, beliefs, ready-made interpretations, and solutions are all set aside in order to focus on the object of the inquiry itself without interference. When we suspend our assumptions and judgments, we move closer to the reality itself and are able to make much more direct contact with our experience. When we objectify our feelings, preferences and expectations about something, we can observe our relationship to a concern as it is, rather than as we think it should be. We become open to our own reality.

This suspension of previous assumptions involves attention, listening and looking at an object and is essential to exploration. This openness exposes reactions, impulses, feelings and opinions in such a way that we can see and examine them in relation to the topic. This suspension, then, allows the external object and our internal responses to be examined as they are. There are several aspects of this intentional suspension.

We hold in suspension all that we take for granted and the common social constructions of how we are and should be. If we want the possibility of awakening a profound sense of wonder and finding the genuinely new in a situation, we must let go of the ways we have interpreted reality. All clichés go by the wayside. We let go of how we have been taught we should feel about something. We intentionally examine the connections and associations that are commonly made about it. When we succeed we are able to be surprised and amazed. We are much closer to our own selves and our interaction with the world. We are better able to discern what is new and fresh in the situation.

We put in brackets all of our current assumptions about a topic. We bracket what we know or think we know about it. It's not that we don't know anything, but that we hold what we know up for examination and do not allow our previous judgments to affect what we actually see. We engage in the inquiry as if there are no pre-existing explanations. We engage in the inquiry so the situation itself can actually speak to us. In order to consciously surface and examine the foundational aspects of a topic, we look at our understanding of reality without the filter of past assumptions. Without the noise of our thoughts, we are able to be much more attentive to reality and more open to discovery.

We hold in suspension our existing knowledge, theories, conclusions and solutions. If an inquiry is to be open, we seek answers rather than beginning with them. We work through the inquiry without knowing the resolution. We enter into ambiguity purposefully in order to form interpretations based on examination of reality. We seek meaning related to the realities we have discovered. The purpose of an inquiry is to explore possibilities for an appropriate resolution.

Metaphorically, we bracket or temporarily step out of our situation in the world and who we are in order to understand it, envision its future and make choices about it. We recognize that we are not fixed entities that never really change. When we do, possibility is open to us in ways that are unhindered by our current grasp of who we are. As we are able to see the world as our construction of it, we are able to generate new ideas, thereby renewing and refreshing the way we understand our world and ourselves. Phenomenologists call this an *ontological reduction.* As Jean-Paul Sartre puts it, we must *nihilate*[9] our current situation and enter into the open, reflective, value-forming and choice-making dimension of ourselves.

More recently, David Bohm, Donald Factor and Peter Garrett proposed the idea of putting brackets around one's views.[10] They use the term "suspension" to describe this activity. The methodology derived from Bohm's work is often called "Open Dialogue."

> *Suspension of thoughts, impulses, judgments, etc., lies at the very heart of Dialogue . . . . Suspension involves attention, listening and looking and is essential to exploration . . . . The actual process of exploration takes place during listening—not only to others but to oneself. Suspension involves exposing your reactions, impulses, feelings and opinions in such a way that they can be seen and felt within your own psyche and also be reflected back by others in the group . . . . Similarly, if a group is able to suspend such feelings and give its attention to them then the overall process that flows from thought, to feeling, to acting-out within the group, can also slow down and reveal its deeper, more subtle meanings along with any of its implicit distortions, leading to what might be described as a new kind of coherent, collective intelligence.*[11]

Radical openness is one of the key conditions for an open inquiry. Without it, the inquiry would be unduly constrained. It would leave us susceptible to believe a certain predetermined thing, live our lives in a way that is already defined or make choices that were articulated, even tacitly, prior to the conversation. It would be like beginning a problem-solving session with an answer rather than a question. Without this phenomenological reduction, we fall prey to ideologies and misuse of dialogue as a sneaky form of persuasion.

Methods of Inquiry

The third foundation of the discipline of phenomenology, methods of inquiry, focuses on the processes used to explore a topic. It combines what phenomenologists call eidetic and hermeneutic reductions. Reduction, from Latin *reducere*, 'to lead back', points to a series of reflective steps that leads one to grasp the core characteristics, meaning and significance of a topic.

Inquiry begins with what is termed a methodological reduction in which each inquiry is viewed and approached as unique and methodological approaches are developed for each unique situation. We begin with the human concerns we are considering and the core questions we are trying to answer. There is no single, universal set of steps to go through. In keeping with the nature of the

---

9 Sartre, 1943, p. 83. *Nihilate* is the English translation of a word invented by Sartre. Not found in any dictionary, it means, "to make nothing" or to intentionally take something out of being.

10 Bohm, Factor, and Garret, 1991

11 *Ibid.* The work of Bohm and his colleagues has done a great deal to popularize the formation of a phenomenological attitude.

discipline, the specific steps, procedures and questions are only found in relation to the nature and purpose of the inquiry itself.

Kierkegaard said, "I always reason from existence, not toward existence, whether I move in the sphere of palpable fact or in the realm of thought. I do not, for example, prove that a stone exists, but some existing thing is a stone."[12] Husserl talks about "being as experience." What he calls the principle of all principles is that "Every originary presentive intuition is a legitimizing source of cognition, that everything originarily offered to us in intuition is to be accepted simply as what it is presented as being, but also only within the limits in which it is presented there."[13] Memory, associative mental connections, imagining and other similar acts of thought can reveal as much about the world as the objective observations and experiences to which they are related.

Thus, both objective and subjective information have real validity within a given contextual framework, and various forms of information must be seen as they present themselves to us. We grasp the world not only through observations from our five senses, but also through our sensual, emotive and relational experience of it. We take all of our observations, perceptions, feelings, memories, associations, hopes, fears and desires into account as we approach any topic. At this stage of an inquiry the focus is on the most basic information needed to resolve the questions we have posed.

A number of additional approaches can take phenomenological inquiry further:
• Imaginative free variation
• Extrapolating possibilities
• Thematic analysis
• Describing or summarizing what has been gained or discovered.

An approach to gaining greater insight into something has been called *imaginative free variation*,[14] in which we examine a variety of related ideas. We take aspects of what we perceive and substitute corresponding alternatives allowing us to see the essential character of our focus.

Extrapolation of possibilities is another approach to discovering meaning in a topic of concern. We step beyond the obvious and imagine what might be possible and generate several options. We try to understand the key aspects of the topic. We pose questions that attempt to isolate and identify the core meaning and significance.

Thematic analysis as a phenomenological approach to qualitative research seeks to discover the essential elements of something. Thematic analysis involves listing all the elements we can discover, coding them into categories, and synthesizing them into themes that together present a whole understanding of the topic in question. An anthropologist or a sociologist may be searching for the core understandings and practices of a specific culture or cultural phenomenon, for example. An educator might do the same in order to discover the ways children learn.

---

12 Kierkegaard, 1936, pp. 31-35
13 Husserl, 1983, p 328
14 Husserl, 1970

Finally, we must actually describe or *summarize* in some form what has been gained or discovered in the exploration and determine the implications. In some cases, the result is pure description of the phenomenon, called a *structural description*. In others, the result may be the selection of an option or the synthesis of several possibilities in one model. Alternatively, it may involve making personal choices or recommendations for policy. In yet other cases, the description takes the form of a literary narrative or a poem or a work of art, as Heidegger suggested in his later years[15].

15 Heidegger, 1963

2.
The Journey toward
ToP Methodology

In human societies there will always be differences of views and interests. But the reality today is that we are all interdependent and have to co-exist on this small planet. Therefore, the only sensible and intelligent way of resolving differences and clashes of interests, whether between individuals or nations, is through dialogue. The promotion of a culture of dialogue and nonviolence for the future of mankind is thus an important task of the international community.

—His Holiness the Dalai Lama[16]

As a body of knowledge, the Technology of Participation (ToP) is applied phenomenology, or what has been called a "phenomenology of practice" or "experiential phenomenology."

Since its inception and because of its content-less nature, experiential phenomenology has been applied to a wide variety of professional fields. With roots in academia and use in research and writing projects in many fields, experiential phenomenology has been applied in many professions as the major approach to their practice. The earliest were psychology and psychiatry, closely followed by education, various aspects of health and medicine, as well as community and organizational development, management consulting and many others.

ToP methodology has been primarily focused on organizational and community development and public consultation, dialogue and engagement. The consistent application of a phenomenological approach led to the formation of a unique methodology through a series of major steps. This chapter traces the formation and development of ToP methods as applied phenomenology.

The human factor

What does it mean to be fully and authentically "human"? This philosophical quest is important to people committed to developing community and humanity, and it was central to the founders of the

---

16 In a speech by His Holiness the Dalai Lama to the "Forum 2000" Conference in Prague, Czech Republic, 4 September 1997, and quoted in Atlee, 2003, p. 277.

Institute of Cultural Affairs (ICA). In this quest a well-known subset of phenomenology seemed to capture a lot of perspectives. Existentialists posed many of the same questions, conceptually and in practical research.

The regions of being

One perspective on what it means to be fully human comes from Jean-Paul Sartre. He broke being human down into two "regions" of being, "Being-in-itself—*l'etre en-soi*" and "Being-for-itself—*l'etre pour-soi*." In talking about regions, he used a spatial metaphor to articulate a mental model of human consciousness.

Being-in-itself – *l'etre en-soi*

> *Being is. Being is in-itself. Being is what it is.*[17]

We are given life and we are exactly who we show up in the world as. Heidegger uses the word *thrown* to indicate it is as if we are randomly catapulted into our given situation. Being-in-itself is our very existence, the totality of our givens at any moment, that which is. It is what it is and does not even have the capacity to be anything other than what it is. It is substantial and real. It is our circumstances—the facts of our lives—the events that happen in our world. It is our history and life experience. It is the objective reality of our lives at any given moment. It's my profile and my history. This is me as an entity; a human person.

In the cartoon "Popeye" the sailor says "I am what I am and that's all that I am. I'm Popeye, the sailor man." He can, in that statement, only see himself as he exists. He is aware that he exists, but rather than reflectively *intend* to be a sailor, he simply takes his givenness as his identity. He makes no claims to self-awareness (self-consciousness), or any possibility of creating himself.

Consciousness in this region of being is directed toward the immediacy of living in the moment. It is not self-reflective and not aware of itself as a consciousness. Our awareness is just itself and limited to navigating our way through life. It can be intelligent and it can be honed through experience, but it is entirely in itself.

Being-for-itself – *l'etre pour-soi*

> *The being of consciousness is a being such that in its being, its being is in question.*

We live in the world in our own situation impacted by the events around us. This happens at the most mundane and specific level as well as, and in dynamical interaction with, a "meta-" or global level. That experience can trigger within us an internal crisis and raises questions for us at the most existential level. We often seek to escape from those questions, and we can take an authentic

---

17 Sartre, 1941, p. 27

relationship to them. Being-for-itself, the self-conscious,[18] relationship-taking dimension of our life is activated. It is non-substantial, fluid, moving and changing in dynamic ways related to the situation and choices we make. It is, as Sartre puts it, a "nothing," in that it is pure possibility. It is pure dynamic activity. Being-for-itself—"*pour-soi*", is the self-consciousness that allows us to transcend the givens of our situation. It is the self-conscious relationship I take to the objective reality of my life. It is, as Kierkegaard says, the relating itself.

If we are to alter our relationship to our situation, our current identity and sense of who we are have to go so that "being-for-itself" can take the stage. It is only being-for-itself that can alter our relationship to our situation. We step into an empty space every time we contemplate, make and act on a conscious choice. We continually recreate our self, our being-ness, all the time. These dynamics of being interact all the time because being is alive. Our being is constantly striving to be a self. As it does, the "in-itself," our presence in the world, changes. It dies and is reborn in a new form. It is the activity of self-conscious living. Sartre says we do this as a "presence-to-self" in that we have the capacity to stand aside from our selves, observe what we are feeling, thinking, doing and choosing as we do it.

So *being-in-itself* is the thing itself, be it the self or something in the world. It is what it is, whatever it is and has its own characteristics and properties. *Being-for-itself* is the attitude or relationship I take to the object of my consciousness. In the ToP approach to phenomenological inquiry, we look at the object of our focus as it is and begin by simply describing what we grasp with our senses. When we metaphorically step back from it, we activate the consciousness of being-for-itself to discover and articulate our relationship to it. We step beyond basic consciousness to become conscious of our relationship to the reality of our focus. This fundamental human capacity enables us to transcend our immediate situation and reflect as a fully aware, self-conscious person.

The dynamics of being

Another of the earliest sources for what became ToP methods came from the work of Søren Kierkegaard.[19] ICA summarized it slightly in this phrase:

18 This is not *self-conscious* in the popular sense of the word but in the phenomenological sense expressed by the work of Kierkegaard, Sartre and others.

19 In Chapter 2 of *The Sickness Unto Death*, written in 1849, Søren Kierkegaard provides this definition of faith: "By relating itself to its own self and by willing to be itself, the self is grounded transparently in the Power which constituted it." Kierkegaard, 1941, p. 147
The fuller and more complicated statement is, "Man (a human person) is spirit. But what is spirit? Spirit is the self. But what is the self? The self is a relation which relates itself to its own self, or it is that in the relation (which accounts for it) that the relation relates itself to its own self; the self is not that relation, but (consists in the fact) that the relation relates itself to its own self." He concludes by saying, "This then is the formula which describes the self when the condition of despair is completely eradicated: by relating it to its own self and by willing to be itself, the self is grounded transparently in the Power which posited it." p. 146

"The self is a relation, which in relating itself to itself, and willing itself to be itself, is grounded transparently in the power which posited it."

The assertion can be broken down into three distinct parts that we can unpack gradually:

• Beginning—The self is a relation,
• Middle—which, in relating itself to itself and willing itself to be itself,
• End—is grounded transparently in the power which posits it.

The self is a relation

I have always thought of myself as a person descended from European peasants, born to a farm family with a certain history, shaped by specific influences, possessing certain characteristics, abilities and beliefs. I have done and said certain things and have formed certain relationships with others. I can be described physically, historically, psychologically and sociologically at any point in my life. I live out of social and cultural narratives, norms and routines. I try to improve my situation by doing things that will alter some of the factors. I go to university, get a job, and build a family. I am defined by the world's standards. That's me in the world. It's me in my situation at any moment. Any perceptive observer can say a lot about me in exhaustive detail. This self is a noun and exists as a fact within a social context.

Kierkegaard begins by asserting that the "self" is a relation which relates itself to its own self, and later in the sentence he says "the self is not that relation, but (consists in the fact) that the relation relates itself to its own self." Another way to say that might be that the self consists in the very fact of the activity of relating to itself. Relating is a non-physical activity that makes connections, forms attitudes toward, and exercises will. So the Self exists in an act of consciousness. The idea that who I am is not a physical person, but an act of consciousness is a lot harder for me to grasp. If I am not the sum of the aspects of my situation, who am I?

I first experienced this when I was about 17. When my father died suddenly, I realized I would have to take on a different role in the family. I was able, with no substantial effort on my part, to view the person I had been, to envision the demands that would be placed on me as the oldest son, and to see that I would need to be different. It happened in a flash and it happened over a period of about a month. The death was the catalyst that activated an existential question, "Who am I?" in my life.

Who asked that question? It was not the "me in that situation". It was my inner self who raised the question about who I was to be and my relationship within our family. I discovered my "self" within myself or, to put it another way, a deeper dimension of myself. Looking back, I can see that I discovered, at that point, that I was free to make some choices, and that I could direct my will from a deeper place.

This kind of "self" is a verb instead of a noun. It is actively changing and being rediscovered at all times, not a defined, static thing. The "self" that I am is a self-conscious, dynamic, living reality that forms intentions. When I reflect on myself in the world, I am metaphorically standing outside my self-in-the-world looking at my self as I am in the world. I can observe my activities, characteristics and experience and the ways I have been with others. I can see what is happening around me and I can sense my own reactions to the events in my life and in the world around me. I like some things. I am fascinated by some and appalled by others. I form certain ideas and make certain choices. The "I" that is the "self" is self-aware and that consciousness is the central characteristic of being a "self". That is the "self" that relates to myself in the world and can move beyond myself as I am now.

Can you see the connection to phenomenology? In that moment of inquiry I was standing in a place of radical openness and intentional focus.

Acts of self-consciousness or self-awareness

Kierkegaard attempts to describe the process of becoming what we might call a realized self. We don't just run out and become a fully realized "self" straight away. There is no instant spirit in a box, just add water, here. For Kierkegaard it is like a play with two acts. He uses *spirit* and *self* as active words, because they represent activities of the self. Our deepest self is not a noun, but a verb. It is not **a** "being" like being a certain thing or a certain person, but "be-ing" like a dynamic ongoing activity or a process. It has two aspects, *attentionality* and *intentionality*.

Act 1: Attentionality—*the self relates itself to itself*

In Act 1 of this drama, the self faces the reality of itself in its personal and social context. We observe and understand ourselves, grasping the realities of our situation and our responses to it. We look at how we react and respond to it. We look at our situation in our family, with our friends, our workplace and colleagues, our profession and career, our life in our community and society. We observe what is happening and gain a sense of our lived experience. We seek to gain a sense of our feelings and attitudes toward our situation. We seek to understand how we have related to the various aspects of our life. We look our life right in the face and acknowledge our situation as it is. It is not an easy thing to do and often takes a lot of time, with plenty of prods, and is often triggered by a crisis or the surfacing of an existential question in our lives. Inasmuch as we do it with honesty, we say yes to our situation. We may not like everything we see or discover, but we acknowledge our situation as it is and grasp the naturally occurring indicatives of our reality. John Baggett, in *Times of Tragedy and Moments of Grace*, talks about this step as "the willingness to face reality."[20]

Attentionality is paying attention to life as it confronts us in our situation. We pay attention, give attention and we attend to our situation. When we examine facts about a topic, we can see each topic and situation as it is. We recall the events and activities in our life experience as they actually happened. We grasp the realities of our situation. We also stand beside our immediate experience to note our reactions and immediate responses, the feelings, connections and associations we naturally make as we are confronted with the reality in our situation. We are exercising our attention.

---

20 Baggett, 2009, p. 105

Act 2: Intentionality—*the self wills itself to be itself*

In Act 2, the self actually embraces reality and, stepping beyond acknowledgment, affirms one's real situation and decides to live in that reality in particular ways. We bring the major pivot points in our lives into alignment. Our foundational understandings become related to every detail of conscious life. Our values are reflected in our thinking, organization and action. We actually intend to be the person we are in the situation we are given. John Baggett calls this act "the grace to embrace reality."[21] We say yes to being the self that is in this situation.

In this act of affirmation we form our most foundational attitudes and intentions toward our real situation in the world. This act forms our will. We make choices and decisions. This is where the deepest "change of mind" takes place. Our most foundational images of the world, our identity and the most core attitudes that shape our decisions and actions are formed here.

This self is free to direct its will. We take it for granted that history is created. We know our actions on a micro and macro level shape our world and our situation. As we develop strategies and approaches to our own life situation, our workplaces and the world's socio-economic-cultural challenges, we catalyze change and see the results. We know it. We see it. We know we are not simply fated to evolve in either a willy-nilly or a specifically predetermined manner. Without directing our will, we flow along with the stream of ordinary life without much reflective self-consciousness, bound by the narratives and conventions of our culture. Life and the self do not need to be viewed that way. Today we know, like we have never known in human history, that we can make a profound impact on the way our world is shaped in the future.

Intentionality is taking a relationship to and taking initiative in responding to life as it confronts me. We are more than beings composed of body, soul and faculties. We are thinking, willing, ceaselessly in pursuit of life in some specific, concrete form. We are forever choosing among a vast array of possibilities open to us at any moment. We are always pursuing our selves, finding ourselves, projecting our self toward a new self that is being forged out of the possibilities of the present. We live in intentionality, in a never-ceasing process of tending toward the future through our choices. Intentionality is grasping life's imperatives and forming them into self-conscious intentions toward our situation in the world. To live humanly is to be in a crisis of decision at every moment.

The always-present capacity for active self-consciousness is a dynamic force that is alive—to perceive, reflect, interpret and make choices. We are that intensified consciousness, that relationship-taking capacity toward our givenness at any moment in any situation. To lead an authentic life, a person must *choose* a life, not live a life merely shaped by the world. To be human is to participate intentionally in shaping one's future.

The self is grounded transparently in the power which posits it

As a Danish philosopher-theologian, Kierkegaard is talking about God. He does not say so directly, nor does he say we must make any specific confession of belief or that we must act in a certain way.

---

21 *Ibid*

His focus is to describe the activity that eradicates despair and gives us authenticity. Indeed, he says we are grounded transparently, without conditions or external justification.

When we go through those movements or processes, we act in ways that make manifest that which gives us life and takes it away. We become authentically and unconditionally connected with, oriented toward and rooted in that reality which placed us in our situation as self-conscious beings.

We step beyond and are unbound from the forces that keep us in a state of separation and despair. We can face our life and our situation with a clean slate. We grasp ourselves as unconditionally accepted as we are and free to make new life choices. Our orientation is toward the future.

Demythologizing

ICA's founders in the Faith and Life community in Austin, Texas, used and developed methodologies of participation through adult education and training work beginning in the 1950s. Their work began in the classroom where the origins of a unique phenomenological approach to teaching and experiential learning took shape. It involved presentations, individual and group study, and group discussion, and was focused on the full cycle of learning, insight, spirit formation and action.

The purpose of mythology is to tell a story in a way that the unworldly and divine appear as worldly and human; to bring the transcendent into our everyday reality. Before Joseph Campbell became famous for teaching us about universal myths, the theologian Rudolph Bultmann[22] worked with sacred literature in an effort to enable people to find real meaning in texts that were written in mythological language based on the worldviews of bygone eras. For people in the 21st century, things like a three-story universe, a snake talking to a woman, fruit that illuminates the knowledge of good and evil, God writing on stone tablets with fire, virgin birth, resurrection, ascension into heaven and sitting on a throne in the sky simply do not compute in a contemporary direct experience of the world. It is equally true for the idea of a rainbow-coloured snake shaping and populating the land, waters and sky of Australia. Can we really imagine Hanuman, a monkey God, flying to Lanka to defeat Ravana, the personification of evil, and rescue Sita, the symbol of goodness and purity? Does it make sense to us in the 21st century that the Sumerian god, Enki or Ea, a fish that sometimes walks on land in human form, created the first human out of mud? Bultmann was very clear that mythologies of all faiths can have relevance and meaning in our moment in history, but that the mythological metaphors often prevent us from seeing that truth in ways we can take seriously.

Bultmann and others created a new method of interpretation or *hermeneutics* in order to understand sacred literature as relevant for people living out of the urban, scientific and secular view of the 20th century world. He used a phenomenological approach to deconstruct sacred literature into layers of meaning in terms of one's life situation, describe meanings in their historical contexts, and demythologize the language and symbols, translating them into existential understandings that have meaning and application to contemporary life. Bultmann's methodological approach to

---

22 Bultmann, 1941

demythologizing drew heavily on the hermeneutical and existential phenomenology of Martin Heidegger. If we are to derive meaning from sacred literature and mythology or, for that matter, any text or work of art, we must go through a process that enables us to find truth that addresses our real, existential questions and illuminates meaning and significance in our lived lives.

Fred Gealy[23], in an essay called "Encounter and Dialogue", suggests we begin our dialogue with sacred literature by first asking what the writer actually says, allowing authors to speak for themselves rather than beginning with our beliefs, assumptions or someone else's interpretation. We let them "have their say." We look for the actual words and phrases themselves.

He then says we need to ask what happened in the story, because much of the world's sacred literature takes a narrative form. We break out the steps taken and find the elements of a given story or passage. What were the events? He calls them "happenednesses." He asks us to look at the historical, economic, political, social and cultural context. What was really going on? We find the objective occurrences and set them in context. We isolate and identify the human dynamics in the story.

His next step suggests that we ask our own questions. In light of what happened in the stories, we surface the questions that are raised in our own very real lives today, the "existential questions" that strike deep into the core of our beings and raise foundational questions about our very nature. These are the questions that do not go away. They trigger an inquiry or a search for the answers that will enable us to consciously shape our lives. We draw relationships between the happenednesses and our own situation. It is easy to see this as two distinct steps: 1) a reflective self-examination, followed by 2) relating our own life experience to the story.

It is only then, Gealy says, that it is appropriate to ask about the message we take from the story or text. How does it impact me in my real situation? How do I come up with answers to the questions I face? How do I determine my sense of identity and purpose? It is these pressing questions that focus the message and make it personal. It is the answers that provide a framework for authentic meaning and significance for each person.

Gealy's insights into applied phenomenology gave rise to ICA's methods, first as study and teaching methodologies and later as the ToP facilitation methodologies. As they evolved, they were applied to all kinds of challenges in organisations and communities. The *technology* in the Technology of Participation (ToP) is the phenomenological method.

Phenomenology as method

Combining the methods used in demythologizing with insights from Suzanne Langer[24], Gealy and others led to the creation of a unique approach to phenomenological inquiry. ToP methods apply

---

23 Gealy, *circa* 1960s. While many specific approaches were taken to this form of phenomenological hermeneutics, Professor Gealy's description is a good example of the process as it has been applied.

24 Langer, 1957

a deep understanding of phenomenology to examine our experience and derive meaning from it through a progression of four deepening steps.

1. The first step responds to a question by enabling a group to look at the most basic data about the topic. It is often called the **objective** level of thinking, because it enables people to look at any reality in an objective manner. It may involve observing an activity, noting the key ideas in an article or generating ideas in response to a question to which people already know answers.

2. The next step explores the associations, connections, relationships and feelings related to the topic and the basic facts of the situation. It may involve examining one's immediate responses to a question, articulating feelings or looking for similar ideas within a larger list. This is called the **reflective** level of thinking, because it enables people to step back from their observation and examine their own responses.

3. The third step examines the significance, meaning, importance, options and implications of their central focus. It is called the **interpretive** level of thinking, in that it takes yet another step back and enables people to make sense of their experience.

4. The fourth step enables people to come to conclusions, form consensus and make decisions. This is called the **decisional** level of thinking because, in whatever form it appears, it allows people to take a conscious and purposeful relationship to their life situation.

In *The Courage to Lead*, R. Brian Stanfield refers to these stages as objectivity, address, exploration, and integration.[25]

This core methodology is a unique approach to phenomenological inquiry and has provided the foundation for many, many applications.

In the next chapter we delve into the technology before a detailed exploration of each of the ToP methodologies.

---

25 Stanfield, p. 207

3.
The Technology
of Participation

A phenomenologist's job is to describe. This is the activity that Husserl kept reminding his students to do. It meant stripping away distractions, habits, clichés of thought, presumptions and received ideas, in order to return our attention to what he called the 'things themselves'. We must fix our beady gaze on them and capture them exactly as they appear, rather than as we think they are supposed to be.

—Sarah Bakewell, *At the Existentialist Café*[26]

Through exposure to ICA's community development in the 1970s, business professionals started to ask if these methods could be applied in their situations. ICA's work spread from the business community to many other fields, including health, education, social services, all levels of government, and voluntary organizations. It was through this work that the Technology of Participation (ToP) methodology took its current form. The terms facilitator and facilitation came into common use in the 1980s. Laura Spencer first named ICA's approach to facilitation as the Technology of Participation in her 1989 book *Winning Through Participation*. This name has been shortened to ToP.

Three critical aspects form the foundations of ToP phenomenology as a discipline: **intentional focus**, **radical openness** and **methods of inquiry**, as discussed in Chapter 1.

Intentional focus

ToP facilitators start out by asking substantial questions about a topic and people's concerns about it. We want to know the intended focus and we want to know what people care about. Their concerns might be issues, questions, conundrums, fears, hopes or the myriad other ways human care surfaces in relation to a topic. We put intentional focus on the topic and people's concerns to discern

---

26 Bakewell, 2016, p 40

what's needed in the meeting. The following four areas help us keep that intentional focus as we plan.

Rational and existential aims

The *rational aim* articulates what the group will know, understand, or decide by the end of the session. When this objective is clear, the group can stay focused on what is important for them. This aim also helps the facilitator create appropriate questions and process to keep the group moving step by step in an intentional direction to accomplish their goals. The rational aim states what the group itself needs, not a result imposed by one person in the group or even the facilitator.

The *existential aim* articulates how the group needs to BE different by the end of the session. It acknowledges the understanding that any intervention affects participants and creates changes in some way, and it helps the facilitator bring careful intentionality to this process while planning the session. In some iterations of the ToP methods, this is called experiential aim or even emotional aim. These terms were used to be more accessible to the public, but they can easily reduce the intent to what the group feels or experiences during the event. The larger intention of articulating this objective, which is to consciously focus the profound impact of the intervention or the change in the group, can be lost through the use of these "easier" terms.

Articulating the core question

Most facilitators begin by stating the topic and asking a key overall question. A meeting about program development might begin with a question such as "What can we do to make this program most effective for our clients?" This core question continues to remind the group of its intention.

Establishing the concrete or tangible beginning point

A tangible beginning point gives the group an objective shared reality to begin with. This is the "ground" that focuses the inquiry of a conversation. It helps banish unshared assumptions, and allows the group to explore their associations and interpretations in relation to something substantial rather than an abstraction.

The concrete or tangible beginning point might be directly related to the aim, such as a policy statement if the rational aim is to "understand the implications of the new policy." Or it might be indirectly related, as when a generic video on safety is used as the beginning point for a conversation whose aim is to "create a safety plan for our workplace." Sometimes the conversation starts with an art form, such as a video clip, story or painting, or with a shared experience, either from the past or one that the group has just experienced. A presentation can also be the tangible starting point for a conversation.

Radical openness

As facilitators, we lead the group to examine the focus of their inquiry as it is without assumptions, presuppositions or expectations. We model how to stand aside and examine conventional wisdom, allowing the group to see life as it is. This stance is manifest in facilitator neutrality and the surrendering of ideas.

Facilitator neutrality

The facilitator maintains neutrality to the content of the meeting and the work of the group. The facilitator may or may not have any knowledge of the topic or any personal interest in the outcome, but does not allow that knowledge or interest to influence the group's work and decisions. The facilitator stands aside from the content, the people in the group, and the choices they will make. The facilitator must also be *seen* to be standing aside from the group's content: participants must be confident that the facilitator will not use his or her position to affect the results of the meeting. The facilitator is a guide who enables the members of the group to observe their situation, reflect on their experience, discern the most helpful directions, and make appropriate choices.

If I as a facilitator think I already understand an organization's situation and major problems, my opinions and current understanding separate me from the real situation as it unfolds. They form an impenetrable fog between the client and me as a facilitator. In situations where we have some knowledge and experience and about which we have formed opinions, it is only natural to believe that the group needs to hear them. Having thought through a topic, I make my own conclusions and it is very tempting to weave a conversation in such a way that participants come up with what I have already determined to be the "right" answers.

In order to listen with openness and hear what is really being said, I have to put everything I know or think about that situation aside. It is not as if I don't know certain things about the situation or have ideas about them. But only when I put those aside can I take in the lived experience of the organization. When I do, I can be attentive to the uniqueness of each situation I encounter. I place myself in an open state of being where I can be truly amazed and see things as entirely fresh and new. I can meet the situation as it actually presents itself. I can practice critical self-awareness. I can see new relationships and patterns of thought. I can discover significance by practicing radical openness.

Surrendering one's ideas

The facilitator's neutral stance models for the group that they also can see beyond the positions and opinions with which they came into the meeting.

"Surrender is an idea first formulated in 1950 and developed ever since. Most succinctly, it means the maximum bearable suspension of one's socialization in a maximal effort to understand something or someone." David Bohm, a theoretical physicist, discussed the suspension of ideas in dialogue in order to create a free flow of meaning between people in communication.[27]

We come into conversations with our own observations, associations, and construction of meaning. Many discussions tend to present and defend the ideas we already have. Suspending our ideas

---

27 Bohm and Peat, 1987

allows us to stand outside them, observe them in the context of others' ideas, and use all of them to create meaning that is larger than what any one of us came into the conversation with.

Methods of inquiry

Following the phenomenological method of reduction (see page 6 - 7) in which each inquiry is viewed and approached as unique and approaches are developed for each unique situation, ToP methods begin with the human concerns we are considering and the core questions we are trying to answer. The specific steps, procedures and questions are found in relation to the nature and purpose of each inquiry. Undergirding these specific procedures, however, is a fundamental process with levels that guide the specific approaches. Sometimes we call this the contentless method.

The levels of ToP methodology

The stages or steps used in ToP methodology have been called levels, because each step takes the conversation deeper into the topic and deeper into the relationship the group takes to it. Each level is a distinct mode of thinking dominated by a particular type of information processing. These levels form the core of ToP methodology. They have been applied in myriad ways. We use the same terminology to explain the steps in the focused conversation method. We use it in other applications as well, but sometimes different terms are helpful in describing the specific steps. Often the first initials of the levels are condensed into an acronym, ORID, as a mnemonic for the four levels.

The objective level

We find the reality and meaning of life in this real, palpable, observable, sensory world. It is right here and now that we live.

We begin with "what is" and create a common foundation of reality for discussions and collaborative work. Each inquiry starts with a tangible beginning point, the "what is." This might be the movie we just viewed or last month's activity report. We might begin with a focus question, like "What are the elements we want to include in this new program?" This step enables all participants to bring their attention together on the most basic information necessary for the discussion. It also allows everyone to participate in the conversation based on the same information.

At this stage in the process the point is to observe and articulate the most basic information about the topic under consideration. We pay attention and perceive what is before us. If we are reflecting on a movie, for example, we look for the characters, the objects, the scenes and lines of dialogue in order to bring to consciousness what is actually present. If we're discussing a discussion about a report, the questions enable the group to bring to their attention what is actually said. Beginning at this level grounds the discussion in reality.

The facilitator's questions are simple, direct and non-threatening. They bring the group's focus to a topic and seek descriptions of reality as indicatives rather than imperatives. They draw people out of their own observation and reflection and into a group focused on a common concern.

Brainstorming is one way to generate ideas in relation to a question. Alex Osborn popularized it in a 1953 book called *Applied Imagination*.[28] ToP methodology often uses brainstorming as the initial step in an inquiry. In ToP methodology, individual silent brainstorming usually precedes group brainstorming, to allow each individual to reach into their own mind for the information before group noise obscures it.

The objective level asks us to examine what is before us and "objectify" our perceptions. We become lucid about what is present to us and we create a foundation for further inquiry.

The reflective level

Along with making comparisons, we make associations and connections among ideas automatically. It's natural and unavoidable. Feelings are triggered by our experiences and perceptions. We remember things. We see connections with other things. These associations and feelings are as substantial as the externally observable data, and must be considered seriously in making decisions. While they may seem more ephemeral than an observation or a well-honed idea, they play a major role in how we approach reality. It's not hard to see that Husserl's thoughts about comparing related phenomena led us to see that there is another area to examine. The breakthrough made by Kierkegaard, Brentano and Husserl was that subjective information must be included if we are to be inclusive in our inquiries.

Our images, memories and feelings reveal valuable information. They open us to the world of intuition, memory, emotion and imagination. Examining our experience makes us conscious, enriches our dialogue and makes it real. It helps us "experience our experience." We are able to articulate the associations, memories and feelings so we are able to relate to the material at the objective level and move beyond it to a deeper, more personal exploration of the topic. Without conscious effort at this level, people can get stuck in reliving what happened and become unable to move beyond emotion. In conversations, this level takes the form of questions that explore this inner world.

ToP calls this the *reflective* level, because it asks us to step back, identify, acknowledge and reflect on our initial perceptions. We bring our associations, memories, feelings and intuitions about something to conscious awareness. They become real and have a life beyond the moment. Identifying and owning our initial responses enables our reflections to inform the relationship we chose to take to our given situation.

The interpretive level

Once we get this far in an inquiry, where do we go next? The phenomenologists say we're looking for "patterns of meaning." It seems quite natural to ask those questions next. Insight arises out of reflection on real experience. The objective and reflective levels prepare us to look deeper into the topic and move closer to answers to the larger question guiding our inquiry.

---

28 Osborn, 1953

Meaning is created out of the mundane encounters in the midst of life. Meaning is something we all have to work at constantly, by thoughtfully reflecting on the actual life we have on our hands. We work through the layers of meaning, purpose, significance, implications, "story" and values to get to the core. We create intentional patterns and connections between elements, either by categorizing or gestalting the data. We consider alternatives and options open to us. A group can develop insight and understandings and they can move forward together. Obviously, each inquiry will be shaped by the specific question that gives it focus.

ToP calls this the *interpretive* level, because it is here that we analyze, gain understanding and determine what is significant. When we create genuinely shared understanding, we are more able to make insightful choices that are the will of the group.

The decisional level

Insight is a fine thing. Ideas move us forward. If processing insight about life is to be complete, grounded and genuinely meaningful, it must move from abstract insight to something more tangible, and it involves projecting that insight out into the future. Whether that insight is practical or transcendent, it must have an impact on our lived lives.

As we decide future implications for action, our reflection connects us to the world in ways that are real. We assume active responsibility for our situation. We make choices and commitments that shape our way of interacting with our situation. In groups, we make decisions and build consensus, so we can move forward together. In some cases, this means making decisions and choices. In others it means placing actions on a timeline or action agenda. Doing so gives concrete form to the resolution.

We call this the *decisional* level. It enables us to develop an appropriate conclusion to a given inquiry. When we make choices, we commit ourselves to a way forward. Well-designed process at the decisional level gives collaborative decision-making real power. In situations where the focus is functional thought such as solving a problem, the term decisional captures the intent of this step in the process. The term decisional is likely to survive as the common name for this activity within the framework of ToP facilitation, but other names illuminate what can happen at this level as well.

When the methodology is used in situations of substantial thought, the generation of transcendent insight. or the activity of consciously forming one's stance toward life, this level has been called *theological* and *symbolic*. Based on Kierkegaard's work, it has also been called the *relational* or *existential* level. Similarly, John Kloepfer has called this level *maieutic*.[29] Derived from the Greek for midwife, maieutic questions bring forth latent knowledge, depth understanding and transcendence. In the specific applications derived from this usage, people are provided with ways to take their insight and move beyond the material, physical plane of this world and connect themselves with transcendent reality.

---

29 Kloepfer, 1990.

The four stages of the contentless method of inquiry provide the foundation for all the specific ToP methods, and allow facilitators to create new methods and designs to meet new situations.

In Section 2 we will explore each of the core ToP methods, including how they form a henomenology of practice incorporating the three aspects of *intentional focus*, *radical openness* and *methods of inquiry*.

Section 2   Core ToP Applications

On the most powerful end of the spectrum (of consensus) is the experience of real "magic" in group process. Beyond the laborious process of hammering out fair and square working agreements, many of us have experienced this magic, a transformational "flow" state, a process of "co-sensing" together the ever-changing "whole picture" as it emerges during a shared exploration of a problem or topic. In this kind of process, agreements are usually experienced as shared discoveries, and arise naturally almost incidentally out of a deep exploration of diversity.

—Tom Atlee[30]

30 Atlee, p 239

4.
Introduction to the
Core ToP Methods

Heidegger is philosophy's great reverser. In Being and Time *it is everyday Being rather than the far reaches of cosmology or mathematics that is most "ontological." Practical care and concern are more primordial than reflection. Usefulness comes before contemplation, the ready-to-hand before the present-at-hand, Being-in-the world and Being-with-others before Being-alone.*

—Sarah Bakewell, *At the Existentialist Café*[31]

To be heard is one of the greatest gifts we can give to an individual in a group.

—E. J. Mings

Applying phenomenology

Since 1988, when ICA moved from a tightly knit global organization to a network of national organizations and individuals, a great deal of creativity has been shown across the world in adapting ToP methods to local cultures and situations. Many variations are used and taught in various locations. To try to pinpoint the core methodology and bring some consistency, a global dialogue took place in the early 2000s. This conversation resulted in the identification of five core methods that define the ToP approach.

The five core methods are the **focused conversation method**, the **consensus workshop method**, the **ToP participatory strategic planning process**, **action planning**, and the method known variously as wall of wonder or historical scan or **journey wall**. The mastery of these core methods, as demonstrated through a certification process, defines a "ToP facilitator." This focus on five core methods does not limit the creativity of how people apply the methodology. However, a deep

---

31 Bakewell, 2016, page 85

understanding of the core of the methodology will allow that creativity to reflect the underpinnings of the phenomenological method.

Toward a pattern language for facilitation

Christopher Alexander, Sara Ishikawa and Murray Silverstein of the Center for Environmental Structure of Berkeley, California described a pattern language for architecture in *The Timeless Way of Building*[32] and *A Pattern Language*[33]. Their key idea was that the "problems" faced by architects and designers can be solved through the use of some basic *design patterns*. When one is designing something like a house, they must solve many design problems. A single solution that works for many situations is called a design pattern. For example, take the problem of how to design the entrance to a home. There are several basic ways or patterns to design an entry. It might have a door with 2 tall narrow windows. It might have a small roof or porch covering it. It might have steps and a simple glass door. Only timeless, tested patterns are included. Each design pattern for entryways is given a name and a general description, an explanation of how it works and when to use it. Many single patterns together form a language of useful design patterns that are related to each other and can be used by designers. They help practitioners look at each unique situation and solve design problems as needed.

The concept of pattern language has been applied in other disciplines, such as software user interface design and engineering. The concept of design patterns can also be applied to group participation, specifically in this case to understand the variations within the use of ToP methods.

The core methodology or pattern provides a solid foundation for the continued development, use and adaptation to specific applications. There is a very tangible and relevant distinction between *method* and *application*. The core methodology is the foundational process of phenomenology. It uses distinct patterns of information processing that enable people to begin to explore a topic at the visible, surface level, move through deeper levels, and reach an appropriate resolution of the inquiry. This methodology is a way of enabling the full processing of information and embodies a unique approach to phenomenology. An acronym that holds this core methodology is ORID, after the four levels, as explained on pages 22-24.

The ToP methodology has been applied in many ways. For example, the core ORID approach is applied as a template of conversation questions, as the underlying structure of a consensus workshop, in the structure of a journey of a group through two days or more of a retreat or problem-solving process, to understand the journey from conflict to reconciliation, to generate a clear presentation, when writing a paper, and for many other purposes.

Each ToP method or application is made up of specific design patterns.

---

32 Alexander, 1979
33 Alexander, Ishikawa, and Silverstein, 1977

The collaborative engineering community, people who design collaborative computer tools, has applied the concept of design patterns to the field of collaborative group work through the use of what they call *thinkLets*.[34]

> *A thinkLet is a named, packaged facilitation technique that creates a predictable, repeatable pattern of collaboration among people working towards a goal. ThinkLets describe and communicate sophisticated, complex process designs in a compact form.*
>
> *A thinkLet is the smallest unit of intellectual capital required to create one repeatable, predictable pattern of thinking among people working toward a goal. In order to achieve a goal, people must move through a reasoning process. To move through a reasoning process, people must engage in a sequence of basic patterns of thinking.*[35]

These thinkLets or design patterns are very basic sets of procedures that a facilitator can use to help a group do a specific task. An easy example is brainstorming in the ToP consensus workshop method. Brainstorming is a distinct thinking process with a simple set of procedures that allows a group to articulate a broad spectrum of ideas in relation to a focus question. There are many specific ways to do brainstorming—each distinct way can be called a design pattern.

ToP facilitators use these basic pattern elements to create many practical applications. They all apply a phenomenological approach. Each of the applications begins with a focus on a specific object, experience or question and proceeds through a phenomenological process to an appropriate resolution. Each has its own results or "product" and those involved in it are enabled to relate to themselves and their situation in a new way. The most obvious are major applications like the focused conversation method (in fact, the acronym ORID is commonly used for the focused conversation method). These ToP applications themselves are built of smaller design patterns like brainstorm and gestalt. In many cases, facilitators draw on not only the major applications, but use the specific design patterns in creating a very customized approach to a specific facilitation project.

The method is the message

ToP methodology does not have a direct content message. It follows Marshal McLuhan's insight in *Understanding Media*[36] that the medium is the message and the content is the audience. The methodology itself, as medium, is the message. "Your ideas are relevant and valuable." "The group needs the best wisdom available to make the wisest decisions." "You can shape your situation and your world." These ideas are integrated into ToP facilitation through a complex of values, practices and application of methodology. ToP facilitators often say these things directly because they are using a methodology that supports them.

ToP methodology provides a process through which an individual or a group can pursue, in

---

34 Briggs and de Vreede, 2009
35 Briggs, deVreede, Nunamaker, and Tobey, 2001
36 McLuhan, 1964

principle, any inquiry. It enables groups to examine their own images or pictures of a situation in relationship to a topic. Each participant contributes, from their own perspective, thoughts relevant to the question at hand. As the group reflects on the compilation of ideas, their picture of the situation grows, develops and changes. They make meaning together.

Forming authentic consensus

A group can form a common understanding and give shape to a common will. This is what we mean when we speak of consensus. It is not necessarily agreement, nor is it submission to stronger voices. Authentic consensus is an expression of the being of the group. The group activates "being-for-itself" and, incorporating its diversity, becomes a single entity in its quest to move forward together as one.

Core applications of the phenomenological method

Currently the ToP global community has identified several applications of the *phenomenological* or *contentless method* that are considered the core of our facilitation practice:

- The *focused conversation method* uses the phenomenological method in the form of a guided discussion.
- The *consensus workshop method* uses it to solve problems, build models and think through major questions.
- The *ToP strategic planning* process uses focused conversations and consensus workshops to enable a group to develop strategy and implementation.
- The *action planning method* uses the method to create practical plans that can be implemented.
- The *journey wall method*, also known as the wall of wonder or historical scan, enables a group to look at its situation and, appreciatively, use it as a stepping stone to the future.

In addition, two core study methods were developed early in ICA's history as a training organization. These are not precisely facilitation methods, but can be used in conjunction with them. They are powerful tools for understanding a paper or a book and connecting it to personal experience.

- The *charting method* uses the phenomenology to deeply understand a book or paper, allowing the reader to have an authentic dialogue with the author and internalize the existential message of the paper.
- The *seminar method* guides individuals in a group to wrestle with a book or paper, grounding it in their experience and allowing its ideas to address their lives.

The focused conversation method

The focused conversation method grew out of the efforts of ICA's founder Joe Mathews in exploring how to use more contemporary, completely secular forms of art and literature to help people reflect on their own lives. The process took the form of a conversation about a poem, story, movie or work of art. The conversation begins with a clear object of focus and explores an individual's perceptions, responses and associations as a gateway to profound reflection on the dimensions of one's own life as illuminated by the particular art form. Developed in the late 1950s, it became known as the *art form conversation*.

One of the stories told about that time was about when staff took inner city youth to see art forms (movies or art exhibits) hoping it would give them a new perspective on themselves and their situation. The youth enjoyed the trips but saw no relation to their lives until the conversation method was used to get them to reflect and relate what they experienced to their own lived experience.

It was this method that most clearly crystallized a unique method of inquiry involving four successively deeper questions. As such, it reveals the core methodology most clearly. Since then, it has been used in a myriad of ways with many and varied beginning points and topics; it is now known as the focused conversation method.

This application of phenomenology focuses on lived experience and its challenges ranging from the most pressing existential questions we face all the way to the most practical problems we are driven to solve in our daily life and work. It has been used within, beside and apart from faith contexts and yet enables the kind of in-depth conversation most often associated with the exploration of faith and a life of authenticity.

The consensus workshop method

Mathews firmly believed that the role of the church is to act out its faith in the world. The workshop method was, perhaps, the clearest step into the world in that it provided a practical way for any group in any context to examine a situation and form practical responses. One of the earliest uses of the method was in the community development project on the West Side of Chicago called 5th City. A group of community leaders and ICA staff met to name the key problems in the community. They started brainstorming problems until three huge blackboards were filled with hundreds of different problems. The group was overwhelmed and in despair. Someone said, "Let's try to cluster similar problems together to see if we can see some patterns that will reveal some root problems." The clustering revealed about 20 root issues, and the group began to have a hope that perhaps they could address them.

A consensus workshop begins with a clear focus question and group members brainstorm responses to that central question. The whole group then clusters similar ideas together. They examine each idea cluster and name the core thought pattern as a distinct response to the question posed. The whole set of responses forms a coherent group response. The group reflects on its work and decides what steps they will take next. Because it enables a group to form a common understanding and a common will, it is now called the consensus workshop method.

Strategy planning and strategic thinking

As ICA's community and organizational development work expanded, concerns deepened for the formation of effective strategy and action. The process of development and the formation of developmental strategy is a complex, interrelated whole that contains specific and very real polarities. At the most general level, there is a tension between the group's vision for the future and the complex of factors that negate the vision or hinder its fulfillment. Seeing the specific barriers in relation to a vision enables a group to see their whole strategic situation and identify key underlying contradictions that must be addressed if they are to realize their vision. Naming those contradictions provides a platform for strategic thinking. This analysis provides insight into steps and strategic directions that can be taken to address the group's situation in an authentic, future-oriented way. When they have identified their strategies, the group can create specific, practical action plans to implement their chosen strategies. This process has become known as the ToP Strategic Planning Method.

ToP action planning rounds out the basic suite of ToP applications. The core of this method includes identifying a desired future state, analyzing the hindering and supporting factors in the present situation, naming concrete commitments given the present reality, generating actions toward those commitments, and timelining the actions with assignments and estimated costs.

The *ToP journey wall* applies the charting approach to time and historical events to enable a group to look at, discuss, create a story of their journey, and learn from their past experience.

The core of the Technology of Participation

These five key methods are just an introduction to the ToP methodology. ICA facilitators apply this body of knowledge and practice extensively in their work with communities around the world and in organizations of all types. Many more specific applications of this foundational methodology have been developed and refined over the years. ICA has also developed programs and courses to enable people to learn and practice these approaches in their own situations.

Chapters 5 to 9 investigate each of the five core methods in detail, relating them to the phenomenological process.

Chapter 10 describes the ToP process for designing facilitated events. It starts with the conversation with the client and the thinking the facilitator does to discern the client's real needs and the best response. Out of this grist the facilitator creates the process that will enable meeting those needs.

Chapters 11 and 12 delve into the two study methods that are core to ICA's methodologies, the *charting method* and the *seminar method*. These methods also apply a phenomenological approach.

5.
The Focused Conversation Method

Our nervous system is at the same time a data-gathering system, an emotional processing system, a meaning-creation system and a decision/implementing system.

—Edgar Schein[37]

First you have to take the work of art seriously by observing carefully what's there, and what's not. Then you have to look just as seriously at what is going on inside you as you observe the art to see how you are reacting, what repels you, what delights you. You have to peel back layers of awareness so that you can begin to ask what it means to you. You must work to create your own meaning from an artwork, or a conversation.

—Susanne K. Langer[38]

In a university classroom discussing Picasso's Spanish Civil War painting Guernica, Joe Mathews asked his students to describe the objects in the painting. Then he invited them to notice their inner responses. "OK," he said, "Now I want you to think about what sound you hear coming from the painting. I'm going to count to three, and then each of you make the sound you hear. Make it as loud or as quiet as you feel it should be. Ready? One, two, three!"—and the room exploded in howls of pain and rage. The door of the classroom flew open and two students from the hallway stuck their heads in, their expressions resembling the faces in the painting itself. In stunned silence, they heard the teacher ask, "Where do you see this painting going on in your life?"

---

37 Schein, p. 63

38 Personal communication between Joseph Wesley Mathews and Susanne Langer, August 1964. She develops these ideas in *Philosophy in a New Key: A Study in the Symbolism of Reason, Rite, and Art* (1942); *Feeling and Form: A Theory of Art* (1953); and *Problems of Art: Ten Philosophical Lectures* (1957).

The results were startling. These students had thought of art as "a cultural thing" or "a decorative object." Now they saw their lives intimately reflected in the art form. They saw the art form as a force challenging their habitual stance towards life. One participant said, "Suddenly I saw that this was making a claim on me. It was saying, 'Wake up and live your real life.'"

Background

In her studies of art and the mind, philosopher Susanne Langer explored these layers of awareness. When we interact with art, we participate in a dialogue that includes the artist, the work and ourselves as the observers. As we look or listen, we observe not only the work of art, but our own interior responses. We take in the elements and we note our surprise, revulsion or delight. Bringing our responses and intuitions to consciousness enables us to feel the experience more deeply and peel back the layers to discover meaning. Joe Mathews discussed these layers of awareness with Susanne Langer in a number of conversations.

In the 1960s ICA colleagues began applying these principles to conversations in classrooms and study groups, as they saw the possibility for the very stuff of contemporary culture to enable deep reflection. Painting, sculpture, poetry, narrative literature, drama and film were all used as gateways to insight, helping people find ways to relate to their own life situations. The conversations guided people through their own layers of meaning.

The **art form conversation** begins with a clear, tangible object of focus—a work of art like a poem, story, painting, sculpture or film—and explores an individual's perceptions, responses and associations as a gateway to profound reflection on the dimensions of one's own life illuminated by the particular art form. People first respond to questions that allow them to observe the art form and articulate what they actually heard or saw, allowing the creator of the art work to "have their say." Subsequent questions give them a chance to look just as seriously at their own responses, feelings, memories and associations triggered by the work, as well as the personal questions that are raised for them. That reflection provides the platform for exploring insight and meaning, leading to deeper understanding and substantial commitment.

After extensive experience with these conversations on art forms, ICA colleagues began to realize that the events that happen to people that they want to talk about are a different kind of art form. We could use the same method for talking about any topic and exploring its deeper meaning and our relationship as human beings to it. Thus the art form conversation morphed into the most fundamental component of the body of knowledge of what is now known as the Technology of Participation (ToP™): the **focused conversation method**.

Brief description

The ToP *focused conversation method* helps people reflect together on any subject. It has been used in a wide variety of situations, ranging all the way from finding the core idea for a marketing strategy to discussing the meaning and personal implications of a movie, a painting or a novel. A series of questions generate a conversation that flows from the surface to the depth of a topic.

Each conversation is tailored with specific questions to move a group through four levels to meet a rational aim or product as well as an experiential or existential aim.

First a context is set, which includes introducing a concrete, tangible beginning point, such as a paper, presentation or shared experience related to the topic to be discussed. Then *objective* questions are asked that draw out observations and data about that concrete object or experience. Next, *reflective* questions draw out participants' reactions, memories or associations that are triggered by that object. Then, *interpretive* questions help people discern meaning as they draw out connections, implications, stories or the significance of the topic, building on the observations and reactions that have been shared. Finally, the *decisional* questions draw the conversation to a close by summarizing, stating next steps, or articulating a profound insight.

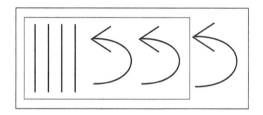

FIGURE 1
Illustration of the flow of the focused conversation method.
Read it as an animated diagram, starting from the left.

Figure 1 illustrates the sentence from Kierkegaard that was discussed in Chapter 2 (see "The Dynamics of Being" on page 13). The straight lines on the left stand for the basic awareness of a bundle of facts about anything in relationship to each other. The first reflexive arrow portrays the awareness of one's immediate internal response to the encounter with the facts: the associations, images and reactions that are triggered by those facts. The second arrow portrays standing back one more step and consciously examining the meaning of the situation, which is built on both the set of facts and the internal reactions to them. The final arrow points back to everything before it and represents taking yet one more step back to name a conscious relationship to the whole situation.

Applications

A focused conversation guides a group to think through a topic clearly together, moving from surface to depth toward a result. Sometimes the outcome is a consensus, but sometimes it is a summary of the exploration of the topic. This deepening journey through the conversation can be transformational.

A common application of the focused conversation method is to develop a shared understanding of a document, such as a policy paper or a useful article. The conversation can help people learn from the document, or apply the content.

Another use is to deeply explore an art form, such as a painting or a film, using it to understand life or one's own life.

This method can powerfully debrief an experience or a series of events, to learn from the past and bring that wisdom into the present and apply it in planning the future.

This method is also useful in solving a problem or a conflict, through creating a shared understanding of what happened, everyone's reaction to it, the implications of the situation for everyone, and a decision about how to address the situation.

The phenomenology behind the focused conversation method

The ToP focused conversation method begins with a specific topic and a tangible beginning point. Beyond that, the content comes from the participants, who bring to the conversation some degree of diversity in their life experiences. The questions move the conversation through stages of perception, response, judgment and decision, which apply the phenomenological method (see "Phenomenology as method" in Chapter 2 on page 17) of starting with what is observed through the external senses, expanding consciousness to the internal response, and then extrapolating patterns of meaning, and finally responding to the situation.

At each level, participants are asked questions to draw them into deeper understanding. The pattern of "surface to depth" runs through each level of the method as well as through the four levels of the method as a whole.

Each of these four levels demonstrates the hallmarks of phenomenology: *intentional focus*, *radical openness*, and *methods of inquiry* (as discussed in Chapter 3 on pages 19-22). These are italicized in the design patterns that follow.

Design patterns and variations

The basic design pattern in the focused conversation method is to follow the four levels or stages in deepening the experience. These levels are often summarized into the mnemonic ORID, objective + reflective + interpretive + decisional.

A whole-system process

This four-stage tool is a total process. It uses all the resources of body and mind to come to terms with the object: the senses, memories and feelings. It uses both intuition and reason. It involves the volitional faculty to push the process through to decisions. In this sense, the focused conversation is a whole-system tool. To borrow a concept from Susanne Langer, the method "subjectifies the outward and objectifies the inward." It imbues what is outside the self with feeling and meaning. Inside, it can bring to the surface emotions and insights, which normally would not see the light of day.

Level 1, the OBJECTIVE level, focuses on sensory information, facts and basic information. This stage is about being aware of the phenomena, or what is going on. The *intentional focus* is directing our consciousness toward what is going on around us. *Radical openness* at this level is not making assumptions about connections or meaning of the phenomena we are observing. The *method of inquiry* at this stage is observation.

At the objective level the focused conversation method uses a number of ways to focus awareness on what is going on.

Observing sensory experience

At the most basic stage the objective level is about observing, bringing to consciousness all of what is going on, or identifying the aspects of a phenomenon. In a conversation, this involves asking questions that allow each participant to share their observations, so they become a part of the experience of the whole group. Depending on what is being observed, the facilitator might ask for visual observations—colours, shapes, textures, sizes, or objects (which may include words or phrases on a page). Or the questions might ask for auditory impressions from an object or experience, such as sounds, words or phrases that were heard. For some situations, questions might ask for physical sensations such as smell, taste, or tactile impressions.

Recalling

Recalling things that actually happened is another element of observation—describing observed events, actions taken, past experience. Participants might recall the parts of a story—the characters, scenes and obvious plot lines, as in "what happened first, next, and then...." Or they might remember the actions actually taken in a project or what happened in an event.

Highlighting facts and thoughts

At this level of the objective phase, a bit of selection begins to surface. People are asked for facts, statistics or basic information, words or phrases that stood out for them, what caught their attention in a paper or presentation, or a list of the elements within a whole.

Grounding in phenomena

Sometimes it helps to name examples of a concept, grounding the abstraction in real phenomena. Describing the aspects of an idea can also be objective information, although explaining the significance of the idea would be at the interpretive level.

Generating ideas

An interesting manifestation of the objective level is getting participants to articulate ideas or thoughts that are already present in their minds. The facilitator might ask for responses to a brainstorm question, or ask people to share existing thoughts or an idea they have been pondering.

Level 2, the REFLECTIVE level, is about associations, connections, feelings and initial reactions. It is about drawing out and articulating the internal responses to what has been observed at the objective level. Here *intentional focus* is directed toward being conscious of our internal responses, and *radical openness* is observing our own responses and those of others without judgement. The *method of inquiry* is observation, now directed inward.

The reflective level can draw out a variety of responses.

Associations

Reflective questions draw out internal reactions and responses triggered by the objective data. Some of these responses are impressions, such as "it seems like X", or "this color—this sound—this experience— reminds me of Y". Or questions may draw out related mental images—"it reminds me of Z" or impressionistic similarities and differences. Questions might also draw out memories (which are more personal and less descriptive than the simple "recalling" of the previous level). These memories can range from experiences, to visual images, to vignettes of their own past experience. Questions may also draw out related ideas, connections, similarities, or themes at a very personal, immediate, or "gut" level. These are not the carefully considered connections or themes at the next, interpretive, level.

Emotions

When appropriate, questions can draw out participants' initial reactions and responses, remembered personal feelings and emotional states, observed feelings and the emotions they saw in others or in literature. Questions can also get people to describe how something affects them or the phenomena under consideration.

Initial attitude

Related to associations and emotions, questions might elicit reactions such as surprise, shock, or confusion, and sometimes bewilderment. Some examples of such questions ask about what is easy or difficult to grasp, or what people like or dislike, or high points and low points, or what part causes shame or pride. Other questions can be about immediate personal connections—what part of this one identifies with, or where they are drawn in, caught up, fascinated, repelled, or intrigued.

Projecting impressions

Approaching the interpretive level, it may be appropriate to draw out worries, concerns, and challenges, intuitions or extrapolations about possibilities or opportunities. Questions may also ask for important or powerful aspects of a phenomenon, or indications of critical elements. As long as these are internal reactions and not yet making definitive statements of value, they are still at the reflective level, and help bridge from reflective to interpretive.

Level 3, the INTERPRETIVE Level, addresses meaning, values, solutions and implications. At this stage, both the external data from the objective level and the internal responses from the reflective level become valuable sources of information that help people understand the meaning of a situation or phenomena. Now the *intentional focus* is about directing our consciousness toward deriving meaning and significance from the external and internal information we have acknowledged in the first two levels. *Radical openness* at this level is about exploration of possible connections and meanings. This is where specific *methods of inquiry* are useful to move towards the aim of the conversation.

The interpretive level of the conversation can involve several elements.

Understanding

Questions of understanding might introduce the interpretive stage. Examples might be "How did this come about?" or "What are the key points of this paper?" Answers at this level are beyond observation alone, and begin to pull together a comprehensive understanding of the topic.

Reference points

Questions might ask participants to articulate their relationship to past events, attempts, knowledge, resources or accomplishments. They might also include comparisons or connections between elements, or to other topics. This stage contains an element of learning, of making new connections to previous experiences.

Exploring meaning and significance

At the heart of the interpretive level are questions of meaning and significance, such as "What implications does this have for us?" "What implications does this have beyond 'us' to the larger context?" "What is the importance of this situation?" "What can we learn from this situation?" "What are the positives and negatives of each option?" Sometimes a question such as "What message might this story have for our situation?" draws out profound insight into the meaning of life.

Purpose and intention

Here questions begin to elicit the "Why" of the situation, such as "Why did this happen?" or "Why would we go in a certain direction?" They may elicit the relationship of a particular proposal to the mission of the organization, or the possible positive and negative impacts of a possible strategic direction.

Toward the future

This stage begins to bridge to the decisional level of the conversation. Questions may elicit lists of options, opportunities or possible solutions. In the case of options, it can be useful to explore the meaning and significance of each option before moving to the next level.

Level 4, the DECISIONAL level, focuses on resolution, direction and action. It draws together all of the information, reactions and exploration of the previous levels. Sometimes it can also draw out the transformational impact of the conversation, if this is the aim. The *intentional focus* at this stage is directed toward summarizing or acting upon the insights explored in the interpretive level. Letting go of previous assumptions, we make decisions in *radical openness* to what we have discovered. The *method of inquiry* is eliciting levels of resolve, both in the sense of commitment and the sense of closure.

It's useful to consider the nature of different levels of decisions.

Resolution

Bringing the discussion to closure is the most surface part of the decisional level. The facilitator might simply draw the conversation to a close, or ask the group to summarize a decision or a consensus that has become obvious through the conversation.

Direction

Sometimes a topic only needs to be resolved with a high level direction, to be planned in more detail later.

Action

If the aim of the conversation is to create action, questions at this point ask the group to articulate what the next steps are. Group commitment to action may be needed, or perhaps individual commitment to action. Questions should elicit the appropriate level of response.

Transformational impact

Sometimes the intent of a conversation is to have a transformational impact on a group, to shake up their world so they can make a conscious change in their operating images or how they relate to each other or to life. In this case, questions can help people articulate a personal insight or what impact the topic or the conversation has on them. Questions that ask people to name an art form, or briefly summarize a situation may help them choose how they are going to relate to it.

Comparison with the design patterns of other methods

The *focused conversation method* is not unrelated to other methods currently in use. It is interesting upon examination that many methods that work well follow the underlying phenomenological method.

Similarities: This method may remind educators of David Kolb's[39] learning theories and experiential learning as well as inquiry-based learning[40]. Readers with a therapeutic background might be reminded of some counseling techniques. Cree colleagues identified a fit with the medicine wheel, as we explored the translation of the method into Cree in Webequie First Nation in 2013.

Differences: A focused conversation is not a totally open-ended dialogue. It focuses on a specific aim and usually has a time limit. But the facilitator does use questions to help group members hold their ideas open to be explored at deeper and deeper levels, consistent with one of the principles of David Bohm's dialogue process[41].

Hints for applying the design patterns effectively

It is necessary to set a context before the conversation begins that establishes a climate of trust and openness in the group. The working assumptions (appendix p. 169) are a good way to do this.

Open-ended questions at every level gather more useful and authentic wisdom than closed-ended questions. A closed-ended question such as "Did you like this?" is likely to get an answer designed to try to please the facilitator, not an honest reaction. And there aren't many options, basically yes or no. "What part of this did you like best?" will get more useful information and evoke a more thoughtful response.

---

39 Kolb, 2015
40 Dewey, 1997
41 Bohm, Factor, and Garret, 1991

Tips for planning the conversation levels

Start with identifying the aims of the conversation. Without the destination of the conversation, the questions are difficult to design and put in order. The rational aim or product that the group needs at the end of the conversation, and the existential aim or how the group needs to be different at the end of the conversation guide what questions you choose to ask.

Then identify the concrete or tangible beginning point. Without a shared tangible starting point (the phenomenon to focus on), the objective questions have nothing to elicit observations about, and the questions and answers will not be objective.

Sometimes a focused conversation is held directly after a presentation or event. It may seem redundant to ask for the objective data—"What points were made in the presentation?" Or "What steps did we just go through?" But if this level is skipped, the group does not have a shared sense of what happened and may base the rest of their thinking on unshared assumptions. At any point, someone's attention wandered, and they missed something. It is not necessary to spend much time at the objective level, but carefully designed questions help the group stay grounded in what's really there.

In Western society, we struggle with articulating the reflective level. Reducing the reflective level questions to "How did this make you feel?" generates very little information, and many people avoid answering. More useful and appropriate information is elicited with several more specific questions, such as "What part of this made you uncomfortable, and which part were you pleased with?" Questions that elicit memories or past experiences can also be very helpful in allowing people to pay attention to their inner experience.

The most successful interpretive questions are specifically crafted to explore insights in relation to the aim of the conversation. For example, if the aim is to understand a policy, one interpretive question may be "What implications might this policy have for our daily work?"

Decisional level questions also work best when they are specific to the aim of the conversation. Sometimes a group decision is necessary, so articulating it is useful: "What have we decided to do?" Sometimes individual decisions are important: "What will you do next to apply what you've learned today?" Sometimes both are needed. Leaving the room without any decisional question will leave the group hanging and unsatisfied. If a decision is not possible, deciding not to decide and when to come back to the topic can be sufficient.

After all this emphasis on the variety of questions that can be used at each level, it's important to realize that you can often accomplish a level with only one or two questions. If your group moves to the next level, that's fine as long as they have satisfied the intent of the previous levels. You don't need to ask all the questions you prepared, if the group doesn't need them. Being able to flex and move with the group means that the facilitator has to be able to discern the levels of thinking in the comments the participants give in response to the questions.

Figure 29 in the appendix on page 170 is a template that will help you plan your conversation.

Examples

These examples of the design pattern and variations range from simple, small, non-controversial topics to complex, important, contentious topics. Sometimes a focused conversation may include blending with other methodologies.

Post-movie discussion: A conversation after a movie is a simple application of the method, where people want to use the movie to deepen their understanding, but no group decision is required.

Book club: When discussing a book that everyone has read for a book club, the conversation can go beyond criticism of the author or the plot to gleaning the wisdom from the book, which can leave participants refreshed and provoked to consider a point of view they hadn't thought of before.

Debrief of a new experiential exercise: After an unfamiliar experiential exercise in an office, the group reflected with questions about the experience and their reactions to it. Then they extrapolated the implications or meaning of the experience, and named how they would apply their learnings.

Response to a management fiat: One group, faced with an unreasonable mandate from top management, discussed the mandate, articulated their reactions and the implications of the mandate, determined what their options were, and made a group decision of how to respond.

Public consultation: Fifty people in a room participated in the same conversation about their previous experience with public engagement simultaneously at each of 10 tables, using questions designed ahead of time. Each table then shared some of their insights with the whole group. The group then built on these insights using the consensus workshop method to come up with a vision for effective public consultation.

Online focused conversations: Exploration is underway on how to use the focused conversation method online, on both asynchronous and synchronous platforms. For instance, the method can facilitate a conversation on Twitter by asking questions one after another, using the ORID format with a small gap of time between them, and providing a hashtag. Participants answer the questions including the hashtag, which collects the answers in the order they were posted. At certain points, someone (or anyone) can look for the patterns of answers and post a summary. Alternatively, the questions can be written on a page in a synchronous online platform and breakout groups can answer the questions and come back to the large group with insights.

Impact of this method

The structure of the focused conversation method can have a variety of major impacts when used with groups. These examples from different settings and purposes may give a sense of its elasticity.

Conversation to resolve a conflict

One colleague received a call from a company, asking him to resolve a conflict. They were in conflict with another company over a particular issue, and they figured it would cost them $10,000 if they couldn't solve it. They wanted to try a short meeting to see if they could move forward. This colleague sat down with the two parties and asked a series of focused conversation questions using the following template:

Clarify the topic:

State the issue in neutral terms. What is the topic for discussion?

Objective data:

What are the facts about this situation? Let's get data from as many angles as possible, especially from the key people involved.

Reflective responses:

Which part of this situation makes you the most upset?

Which part of this bothers you the least?

What past experiences did it bring to mind?

Interpretive insights:

What are possible causes of this situation?

What are the implications of this situation for each person involved?

What are the larger implications that this situation might have?

What are some possible solutions we might explore?

What are the pros and cons of each of these solutions?

What values do we need to hold in a solution to this situation?

Decisional choices:

How might we weave these together to form a solution we can all move forward with?

Someone write down our solution and read it back to us.

Is this our decision?

How shall we implement it?

Within an hour the group had resolved their conflict. They saved $10,000 by imposing a little discipline on their thought processes using the focused conversation method.

Little Miss Muffet

Once when I was young and naïve, in the summer of 1972 at Lake Geneva, I was a counselor at a summer camp. I had teaching experience, and here my "class" was a group of 4-year-olds. I had been using the art form or focused conversation method in my teaching, so I decided to try to use it with these little ones.

I decided to start with the nursery rhyme "Little Miss Muffet". First we said it all together:

> "Little Miss Muffet
> Sat on a tuffet,
> Eating her curds and whey.
> Along came a spider
> And sat down beside her
> And frightened Miss Muffet away."

First, I asked them who the characters were. Easy: "Miss Muffet and the spider." Then I asked them what words they didn't understand and explained that a tuffet was something to sit on (like a tuft of grass), and that curds and whey were cottage cheese. Then I asked them what happened first, next, and after that. They responded with the stages of the plot.

My next questions were "What does this remind you of?" and "Where has something like this happened to you?" I got several stories of spiders and ants in their tents, and other scary surprises. There were also a few tough-kid stories of not being afraid.

Then I asked, "So what is this story about, for you?" There was a short silence. Little Dana Caruso looked blank for a minute, then her eyes lit up. "It's, it's about when something scary happens, you can decide whether you are going to run away or not! And, and, next time I'm going to think before I run away!"

I didn't even have to ask the final question, "What will you do differently because of what you've learned from this story?" —she had already answered it.

Now Piaget would say that 4-year-olds could not think at this level. But when you ask the questions in order, it is like peeling back the layers of an onion, and even small children can take a step deeper in understanding.

I often use this story when I'm teaching adults how to use the focused conversation method—I have them answer the questions as themselves (what it reminds them of often includes situations like when a really scuzzy sort sits down next to them in a bar), and then I tell them how the 4-year-olds answered it. The power of the method to unlock deeper thinking becomes clear to them.

Conversation about how to accomplish the impossible

In the midst of a training session, the assignment was to create a conversation for a real-life situation that was coming up. One manager balked because she had a team who had just put out everything they had to complete a project on time and on budget, and they had postponed their holidays until Christmas.

It was now October, and no sooner had they finished the project than management had assigned them a massive new project that would take them more than full time to finish by the March deadline. She was clear that doing this project and cancelling their holidays would burn out the team. She said, "We can't have a conversation about whether we should do this project—we'll all get fired!" I asked her if the mandate required them to cancel their holidays. She said no, but it would take more than full time work for everyone. So we talked a bit, and she decided that her rational aim was that they would decide "how to humanly carry out this inhuman mandate".

They started with the actual memo from management as the concrete beginning point. She asked what words or phrases stood out for them. Then she asked what worried or upset them about this mandate, and also what was intriguing or exciting about this project. Then they explored the positive and negative implications of doing it. Finally, they decided to work 16-hour days and keep their holidays. Some could have decided not to work for the company any more! But they were able to come to terms with the situation they had, and create the solution that was best for them.

Achieving authentic consensus

Because the focused conversation begins with consciously observing shared reality and articulating what it looks like, and then asks individuals to articulate the range of their internal reactions to that reality, the group's interpretation of the situation and the decision it makes are created from their diverse perspectives on reality. In this process "the whole is truly greater than the sum of its parts," and the result belongs to the whole group. Consensus in this case is not agreement, but it can involve the commitment to support what has been created through the process.

Conclusion

The focused conversation method works because it is built on a natural way of thinking, and helps the group to go deeper step by step. When the conversation is designed well, the group often starts to answer the next question just before it is asked, as the natural process of thinking unfolds.

This method is perhaps the most versatile of all ToP methods. It also most directly reflects the phenomenological method. It can take a group seamlessly through observing the external reality, becoming aware of their internal reactions to that reality, exploring the meaning of the situation, and choosing their responses to the whole situation.

Practical resources

For more detailed information on designing and leading a focused conversation, we recommend *The Art of Focused Conversation* and *The Art of Focused Conversation for Schools,* or the Group Facilitation Methods course[42].

---

42 http://www.ica-associates.ca/product/group-facilitation-methods/ or see http://www.ica-international.org/ica-worldwide to find training in other countries

6.
The Consensus Workshop Method

When people align their individual intelligences in shared inquiries or undertakings, instead of using their intelligence to undermine each other in the pursuit of individual status, they are much more able to generate collective intelligence.

—Tom Atlee[43]

An organization was struggling with their future direction. Each person had their own unique ideas, and they had spent many hours arguing about the differences in their visions, reaching an impasse. They asked a ToP facilitator to help. After talking with the group the facilitator designed this straightforward focus question: "What do we want to see going on in our organization in five years?" After they brainstormed all their ideas, clustered them, and named the bigger patterns of their common vision, they reflected on what they'd come up with. They could now see how each of their unique ideas contributed to a larger vision of the organization, and now each person was able to support the whole vision, not just their piece. One person said, "I thought I was the only one! Now I see that there are others who think like me!"

When a group needs to bring their ideas together to create new insight and find agreement, a consensus workshop can help. Where the *focused conversation method* is intended to probe meaning and insight, the *consensus workshop method* looks for shared patterns behind diverse ideas and perspectives. One of the primary assumptions of this type of workshop is that each of the participants has wisdom to contribute.

Background

The consensus workshop method was originally developed as a way to make sense of a long list of problems and possibilities on a blackboard. The Institute staff and residents of the Fifth City neighbourhood on the west side of Chicago were discussing all the issues in the community that needed

---

43 Atlee, 2003, p. 55

to be addressed. As the list on the blackboard grew longer and longer, reaching several hundred problems, participants were overwhelmed. Someone said, "Let's see if we can find some patterns" and asked the group to put symbols beside items that had a similar root cause. They narrowed down the number of root issues to a reasonable number to handle, and at the same time nothing was left out or marginalized. Everyone's idea was honoured, and the group mustered the energy to address the root issues.

Later on, when flipcharts came into use, they replaced the blackboard, but the need persisted for a way to put similar ideas physically next to each other to make seeing patterns easier.

The use of cards stuck to a wall with tape was the next evolution of the method. Sticky walls, which are nylon parachute cloth sprayed with repositionable adhesive and hung over a wall, made it easy to use half sheets of paper while protecting the wall. Some facilitators use reusable sticky tack or adhesive putty to stick cards directly to a wall, while others prefer sticky notes.

Brief description

The consensus workshop method has five essential steps:
1. setting a *context* that includes a focus question
2. *brainstorming* answers to the focus question (individually and then as small groups)
3. *clustering* the ideas together iteratively to create larger patterns
4. *naming* the patterns
5. having a conversation about the results that leads to *resolve*, often a consensus

Imagine that each person holds a piece of a puzzle that is yet to be put together to create a larger picture. The content of each puzzle piece as well as the relationships between them create the larger picture that no one person came with, but includes all of the individual pieces.

Figure 2 portrays the flow of the process, although it does not strongly emphasize the critical point that clustering is completed before naming.

Purpose

The workshop method elegantly gathers a wide spectrum of ideas from a group, bringing them together to create a larger product that includes all the ideas. The rational aim varies widely according to the content results the group needs, but the existential aim is generally that each person will experience that their ideas are valid and necessary to create a whole picture, idea or understanding larger than they came in with. Each also experiences that they have been heard and that they have heard others.

Here are some specific purposes the consensus workshop is well suited for.

Creating a consensus about core answers to a question

The workshop focuses on a question that's important to the group, such as "What are the competencies of a successful facilitator?" Each participant reaches into their own experience and brainstorms answers, which are clustered together to reveal a list of five to nine inclusive competencies, which they name. The resolve stage can then prioritize these competencies.

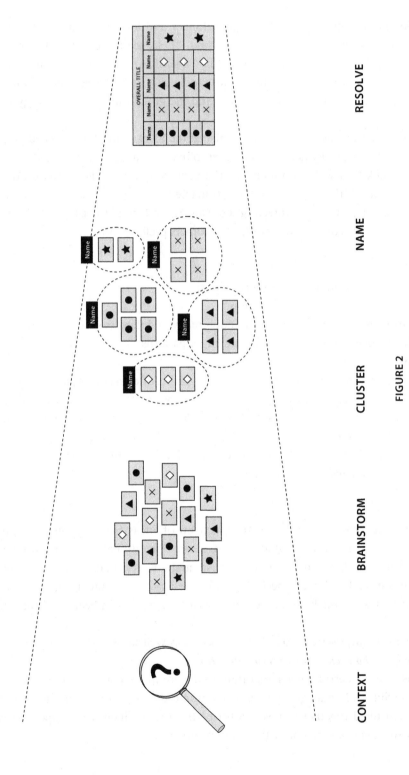

FIGURE 2
Consensus workshop flow

Visioning and strategic planning

The workshop method can be used more than once in succession, first with a focus question such as "What do we want to see in 5 years?" to create a common vision for a group. The second workshop then brainstorms blocks that are clustered to reveal underlying contradictions, which are then named. In the third workshop the group brainstorms actions to address the contradictions, and clusters them by "similar actions" to create powerful strategies to address the contradictions and move toward the vision. For a detailed explanation of this approach, see the Participatory Strategic Planning chapter, starting on page 66.

Creating the core elements of a model or solution to a problem

A focus question such as "What are all the elements of our service delivery model?" allows individuals in a group to brainstorm from their personal points of view. Then the group can bring the wide variety of perspectives together to create the core elements of a model. Afterwards, participants can create and perhaps draw a visual of a model that holds all the named core elements. Using the workshop process allows consensus to be built from diverse beginning points.

Discerning core elements of a project to assign to work teams

In the creation of a project charter, a group can brainstorm elements that are necessary to complete a project, cluster them by what tasks can easily be done together by a team, and name the project elements. Then, at the resolve stage, their part of the project can be achieved.

Naming the core values of an organization

The core question for a values workshop is something like "What values do we want to uphold and see reflected back to us through everything we do?" Some creative sub-questions will help people brainstorm some content-rich answers, such as "What do you believe *about*...teamwork, collaboration, communication, recognition, respect, accountability, productivity, things we would *never* do, things we'd *always* do, etc." Clustering and naming these values with names rich in imagery such as "putting the child's needs first" will answer the focus question with meaningful consensus on core values. The answers can then be formed into sentences or phrases that complete the phrase "As an organization, we value...."

The phenomenology behind the consensus workshop method

Let us step aside for a moment to discuss an approach that has become integral to ToP methodology as a way of processing objective, reflective and interpretive information. We have used the term gestalt to identify the process of relating ideas that respond to a focus question in similar ways. Max Wertheimer, one of the founders of the Gestalt approach, says gestalt is:

> *A physical, biological, psychological, or symbolic configuration or pattern of elements so unified as a whole that its properties cannot be derived from a simple summation of its parts.*
>
> *...the essence or shape of an entity's complete form*[44]

---

44 Wertheimer, 1924

The gift of Gestalt

The focal point of Gestalt theory is the idea of relating specific elements to see a pattern of thought. The "whole" we see is something more structured and cohesive than a group of separate particles. Wertheimer says:

> *There are wholes, the behaviour of which is not determined by that of their individual elements, but where the part-processes are themselves determined by the intrinsic nature of the whole.*
>
> *When a group of people work together it rarely occurs, and then only under very special conditions, that they constitute a mere-sum of independent Egos. Instead the common enterprise often becomes their mutual concern and each works as a meaningfully functioning part of the whole.*[45]

Michael Polanyi addresses this in his book, *The Tacit Dimension*[46]. Polanyi identifies two terms of tacit knowing: proximal and distal. The *proximal* or the term nearest to us refers to the particulars of a situation. The *distal* term, furthest from us, is the whole. The relationship between the proximal and distal terms of tacit knowing has three aspects: functional, phenomenal, and semantic.

In the *functional* aspect of tacit knowing we move from the specifics to the whole. In the *phenomenal* aspect we are aware of the specifics as we look at the larger question. The *distal* term is the larger topic and the big picture questions that elicit specific responses. The *semantic* aspect comes into play when certain relationship specifics are perceived and an overall image is formed. This is the intuitive nature of gestalt. We see the larger picture as we see patterns in the specifics. The phrase "The whole is greater than the sum of the parts" is often used when explaining gestalt. Indeed, this phrase is often stated as one of the foundational assumptions underlying ToP methodology as it is used with groups.

Gestalt in this context is about seeing "'patterns of meaning" in a whole set of ideas given in relation to a specific question. The individual responses to the focus question will, if the focus question is well-designed, be comprehensive in addressing the question. The task is to discern the major themes of thought or distinct answers to the given question. There may be many connections and associations among the ideas. There may be causes and effects. There may be words that are similar or seem to have similar meanings. The key factor in distilling useful meaning from this process is the question used as the guide, the focus question. It focuses the generation of ideas and guides discernment of the thought patterns of the responses. The question becomes the fundamental reference point for a whole inquiry and all of its parts. The patterns are named as the group's response to the focus question.

It must be understood that this is a process of synthesis rather than analysis. One of the easy temptations in performing this process is the tendency to sort elements into categories that are already integrated into our understanding even if they are not consciously identified. It is, without question, much easier for both the participant and the facilitator to sort into known categories, but

---

45 *Ibid*
46 Polanyi, 2009 p. 18

sorting only organizes previous ideas, and does not create new ideas. Analytical methodologies play a necessary role in processing ideas when an overall framework is already firmly in place.

Consistent with the nature of phenomenological inquiry, a true gestalt does not make any assumptions about the relationships among data. Those assumptions are intentionally bracketed by the method until later in the process. There are no categories until they are identified and named. Gestalt—and all phenomenological inquiry—are oriented toward forming new understanding. If the process merely categorizes elements using typologies of information, a true "gestalt" has not happened. A gestalt creates a new picture and a new understanding of a given reality.

A four-step process

Performing a gestalt is a four-step process. The first step is the question posed to a group. That question becomes the focus and reference point for the whole process. The group responds and the ideas are recorded graphically. In the ToP lexicon, this is the objective level of processing ideas.

It is then that the gestalt process begins more formally. The second step is identifying the themes or patterns within the responses in relationship to the question itself. It is necessarily an iterative process which enables a group to formulate meaningful clusters of similar responses to the focus question. Clustering starts with intuitive, reflective associations between responses and gradually builds interpretation of what is emerging.

The third step is to articulate the nature of each identified thought pattern and the relationships among them. This step reveals the group's major answers to the question. When all of the themes are named, the group has created a new image of their response to the question.

For many, this is an almost magical event. The gestalt moves the information from individuals' ideas to the ideas of the group. In a very real way, people give their ideas to the group and they become, to use an economic metaphor, the property of the whole. It is a gifting or a kind of surrender. From a long list of ideas that respond to the question in different ways, the group creates a meaningful understanding of its response to the question. They have discovered their commonality of thought and within it, the major elements.

To wrap up the process, the fourth step, a reflection on the resulting gestalt brings the group to the point of resolution.

Design patterns and variations

Each step of the workshop is carefully designed to unfold inquiry through the application of the phenomenological method: intentional focus, radical openness, and methods of inquiry, as discussed in Chapter 3 on pages 19-22.

Context: *Setting the stage*

The context prepares the group to direct intentional focus on what exists, letting go of assumptions and becoming open to what will be created in the process. Stating working assumptions or ground rules establishes an atmosphere of respect that allows people to be radically open to each other.

1. Explain the product and outcome
Sharing with the group what the process is going to produce helps the group focus, and confirms that everyone has the same intent.

2. Outline the process and timeline
Quickly summarize the steps that the group will go through and the amount of time intended to get to the final product. The group can support the facilitator in keeping the process moving forward. This is also the time to rehearse the working assumptions or ground rules for how the group will work together during the process.

3. Highlight the focus question
The focus question is the key reference point for each step in the whole workshop. It needs to be open-ended: not "What is the best solution to this problem?" but "What are some elements of a solution to this problem?" Prepare the question carefully ahead of time to ensure that it will generate the brainstorm needed to create the results. Write the focus question where the group can see it throughout the workshop, say it aloud at the beginning, and remind people of it when clustering and naming the groups.

Brainstorm: *Generating new ideas*

The brainstorm step focuses attention on the ideas that already exist within the minds of the participants, which are the initial articulated phenomena. Writing the ideas allows them to be externally observable. The *method of inquiry* at this stage moves from individual solitary thinking to sharing ideas with others. Individual brainstorming is critical to ensure that each person's honest and real answers have a space to be articulated before they are influenced by others, and the small group brainstorming helps clarify and refine the ideas before they are shared with the whole group.

1. Brainstorm individually
Ask each person to individually make a list of their answers to the focus question, to allow the uniqueness of individual thought to be accessed and observed. If necessary, add some comprehensive sub-questions to broaden individual thinking—for example, if the focus question is about facilitator competencies, suggest "behaviours, attitudes, knowledge, beliefs" as areas to catalyze brainstorming. Emphasize that there are no wrong answers at this stage.

2. Select your best ideas
Ask each person to mark a few ideas that are their best answers to the focus question. Emphasize that this does not rule out the other answers, but makes sure they include their most important ones.

3. Brainstorm as a small group
Break the large group into small groups to share ideas and to write their ideas on cards. These may be pairs, or threes, or even small table groups. Emphasize that the goal is to include each person's ideas. Suggest a first round where each person says a different answer and write each on a separate card, then add cards for any other ideas that have not yet been captured. The number of cards from

each small group will differ depending on the total number of people in the workshop: you'll need at least 35 total cards to get enough diversity to create consensus, and you will find that about 60 cards total is all you need for comprehensiveness and validity of results. Beyond 60 ideas you will get mostly overlap.

Cluster: *Forming new relationships*

Clustering is the major stage where the activity of gestalt takes place. The *method of inquiry* here is synthesis, looking for larger patterns within the data. *Radical openness* allows new patterns to emerge, and old ones to be reviewed.

1. Gather ideas from each group

Start by getting a few cards from each small group – in one or two rounds, get approximately 15 different cards. Use directions to get a diversity of content from groups, such as "your clearest card" or "the card you're most passionate about". Place them on the wall randomly, usually toward the bottom of the wall to allow space to work above them. Read each card out loud as you place it on the wall.

2. Develop clusters

Start by asking the group to identify pairs of cards that go together to create a similar answer to the focus question. Put a symbol with each pair to prevent sorting or categorizing. For best results, make four or five pairs first before allowing the group to add more cards to a cluster. Then begin to add more cards to the clusters. Remind the group that each cluster will be one answer to the focus question, and refer back to it to ensure that that the emerging gestalt is creating answers to the focus question.

3. Relate extra cards

Ask the small groups to look at the cards they have left, and mark the cards that are obvious overlap with the symbol where they belong. Then have them send up all cards that are *not* obvious fits. These are the cards that will create new ideas, either with new clusters or by transforming the larger ideas behind clusters that are already on the wall. Have the group say where to cluster these, reminding them of the focus question that they are answering. Finally, put up all the cards that are marked as obvious overlap. Every card should now be on the wall.

Name: *Discerning the consensus*

At the naming stage, the *intentional focus* is directed at summarizing the insights that have been created during the clustering stage.

1. Discern the focus of each cluster

This step generally provides an overall instruction that the next two steps carry out, but on occasion it is useful to quickly put a holding phrase at the top of each cluster to guide the group's thinking.

2. Discuss the cluster for clarity and insights

Using the focused conversation method, focus on each cluster one at a time.

Objective: Read the cards in the cluster aloud.

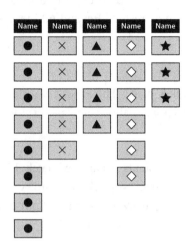

FIGURE 3

Cards clustered in columns on a wall

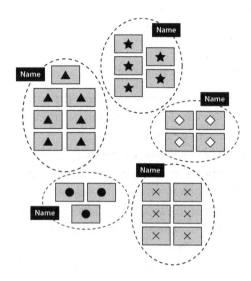

FIGURE 4

Cards clustered by clumping on a wall

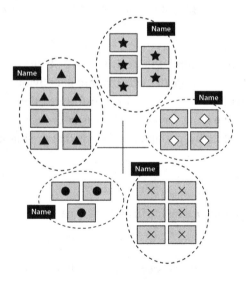

FIGURE 5

Cards clustered in a polar gestalt

FIGURE 6

Strategy cards clustered in boxes,
with the strategies aligned in rows
as strategic directions

Reflective: Ask "What words on the cards in this cluster jump out at you?"

Interpretive: Explore with the group – "What insights into an answer to the focus question are revealed by this cluster?"

3. Name each cluster

Decisional: Ask the group to summarize the insight in a phrase that answers the focus question.

It might help to suggest a grammatical form that will answer the question – for example, if the focus question is "What can we do to…?" then it helps if the answer is in the form *Verb + object of the action*, such as Start new businesses.

Resolution: *Confirming the resolve*

At this stage, the *intentional focus* is on connecting the results of the workshop back to real life. You may want to summarize the results with polished prose, create a visual summary, or name next steps in application or implementation.

1. Lead a focused conversation on the results leading to a resolution

This conversation is tailored to the rational aim and the focus question. The conversation might lead to naming priorities, or it might draw the identified elements together into one solution that holds all the elements.

2. Create a product from the consensus

There are a variety of ways to create a product, which are chosen in relation to the rational aim. The product might be simply a verbatim document of the cards on the wall, or a drawing or chart of the results. Sometimes a group takes vision elements and writes a vision statement, or creates a comprehensive model incorporating all the core elements. Sometimes if the results are strategies, the strategies are put on an implementation timeline, or people are assigned to carry out the plan.

3. Reflect on the experience

Hold a quick focused conversation (ORID) that allows the group to recall what they have just done, acknowledge their varied reactions to it, articulate the impact the experience has had on them as a group, and state their commitment as they move into the future.

Design pattern variations

Flipchart method

In the simplest form of the consensus workshop method, individuals do a silent brainstorm, writing ideas on their own paper. Then the facilitator goes around the table and gets one idea at a time from each individual and writes each idea on a flipchart or whiteboard using the individual's own words. Clustering is done by putting symbols beside similar items on the list. Naming is on a separate page. This is best used for a small informal group, and simple non-controversial topics. It is a great method for a quick topic. A disadvantage is that each person has to speak their idea out loud in public, which can be difficult or embarrassing for some people and cause them to self-edit before speaking. This can limit the authenticity and diversity of contributions. The immovable list of ideas means that when people are looking for patterns, the visual separation of similar items makes them diffi-cult to see. The fact that the facilitator is doing the writing can also lead to misuse of "the power of the pen," when the facilitator (unconsciously or consciously) writes only what they hear, not neces-sarily what people say in their own words.

Card method

The card method is the best approach for large groups of up to 60 people, and for controversial or difficult topics. After the individual brainstorm, small groups share their ideas and write each unique idea on a separate card. There is a level of privacy in this process as participants' ideas are written and submitted by a group, rather than an individual. Also, the ideas are written by the people who own them, so there is little opportunity for the facilitator to skew their ideas. Clustering is easier, because moving similar cards together uses visual connections to help see similar patterns. The facili-tator can help the group explore different possibilities by holding a card in proximity to different clus-ters before deciding. The process sometimes takes longer and seems more formal than the flipchart method. You also need a flat blank wall where you can stick things and that everyone can see.

Visual forms of clustering

There are different visual ways to cluster cards on a wall. The simplest is to put similar ideas one below another, creating columns of similar ideas. This is clear and easy, but can lead to sorting rath-er than gestalt, because it's easy to mistake the top card in the column for a category title. When this happens, new insight does not emerge.

(*Figure 3: Cards clustered in columns on a wall*)

Cards can also be clustered in clumps on the wall. This approach starts off messier, but no card is at the top, so it can support the process of gestalt.

(*Figure 4: Cards clustered by clumping on a wall*)

The polar gestalt was inspired by Buckminster Fuller's discovery that if you look at the globe from the North Pole, all the peopled continents are connected to each other. If you put a circle or perhaps a clock face in the center of the wall and cluster things around it, you can see the connec-tions between separate clusters.

(*Figure 5: Cards clustered in a polar gestalt*)

If you have actions or strategies that are aimed toward the future, you can cluster strategic actions in "boxes" made with square pieces of flipchart paper, and then move the "boxes" into rows of alignment with each other to create strategic directions, adding an arrowhead that describes the direction that they are moving in.

(*Figure 6: Strategy cards clustered in boxes, with the strategies aligned in rows as strategic directions*)

Informally clustering on a table or wall with everyone moving stickies

If there is not much data, and the group is small and well-balanced, this can work. However, with a larger group, there is little discussion about why things go together, and there is no opportunity to create depth insight. It is also possible for the more physically assertive people to take over, and others to back off and let them dominate. When some people can dominate the emerging patterns, the workshop cannot create consensus.

Comparison with the design patterns of other methods

Many workshop-type approaches start with brainstorming. The important thing is what happens to the brainstormed items. The consensus workshop method treats brainstorming in a unique way.

Brainstorming

The consensus workshop method addresses "groupthink", which is often cited as a drawback of group brainstorming and ideation, by providing individual time to think and prioritize one's own ideas silently before discussing them. By not stopping at the brainstorming level, the consensus workshop method uses the initial thoughts of individuals as building blocks to build larger meaning.

Categorizing and sorting

Western thought emphasizes and teaches analysis, sorting and categorizing from an early age. On Sesame Street they ask, "Which of these is not like the others?" It is easy to create categories and sort ideas into them, but no new knowledge or understanding is created, and "miscellaneous" categories are created, effectively marginalizing ideas that are different or outliers. In contrast, the consensus workshop method is best used to synthesize new ideas from a diversity of individual ideas. This approach completely sidesteps the question of agreeing or disagreeing with someone else's idea; it asks how each unique idea can contribute to something the group has not seen before.

Brainstorming and prioritizing

Prioritizing is often done with dots. This process rates some people's ideas over others' ideas and discards any that don't get enough votes. The results stay at the superficial level, never allowing a conversation about how each individual idea enriches a larger picture or deeper meaning. Ranking at this point in the process rewards familiar ideas and often rejects odd but innovative ideas that might usefully add new wisdom. Many people end up feeling that their ideas are rejected or not really heard.

Remote workshops

Although any of these classic ways of conducting a workshop can be used in face-to-face situations, some workshops need to include people in many locations simultaneously, and it's worth experimenting with software to help. The biggest challenges are finding a platform that allows for clustering individuals' ideas without first assigning categories to put them in, and allowing discussion while clustering. Electronic applications for using the method online include Spilter and Stormboard, which mimic sticky notes on a wall; Blackboard Collaborate, which has a whiteboard and moveable text boxes, and Adobe Connect, which uses interactive pods. One colleague uses a desktop-sharing application in conjunction with MindJet, a mindmapping application, to cluster ideas. The mindmapping application can also be projected from a computer onto a screen in a face-to-face meeting. Software can also be useful in recording or reporting on a workshop. The possibilities will continue to evolve.

Impacts of this method

Use of the consensus workshop method has major impact on both the results a group creates (rational aims) as well as what happens to the group through the process (existential or experiential aims).

"There are other people who think like me! I thought I was the only one!"

This comment is heard frequently after a consensus workshop, because the workshop does not ask about agreement or disagreement, but asks how each person's idea adds to the whole that is created together. When no one card or idea stands alone to create the group's results, participants see the other ideas that connect with their own.

Bringing community ideas together from diverse or opposing groups with common intentions

The city council of a major city that distrusted community consultation went through a consensus workshop where they came up with their own ideas about a vision for their city. They then compared their results with what citizens had come up with in consensus workshops in public consultations, and discovered that they were very similar. The citizens had a couple of elements that the council didn't have, and councilors agreed to adopt them. "We missed that and we should add it to our vision!" The resulting vision guided the city for 10 years.

A large First Nation wanted to align their self-governance more with their values. After much consideration, they came up with a question that their citizens could understand and contribute to: "What values do we want to hold in governance?" One thousand people participated in the consensus workshop process in 43 focus groups, and the results were pulled together by a representative group of leaders to identify a consensus on 13 core values for governance. These values formed the foundation for negotiations with their province and the federal government, and for exploring changes to their internal government systems.

A work group with a previous manager who suppressed and punished their participation was suspicious of a new manager who asked for their participation. When they silently brainstormed and then wrote their ideas on cards in small, safe groups, suppressed anger came out on the cards. Asked for clarity, no one owned up to writing some of these cards. When the cards were not thrown out, but clustered to help reveal a deeper insight, participants began to relax and trust that their ideas would be heard. A follow-up session with the group revealed a major shift in trust and positive participation.

Achieving authentic consensus

The facilitator's own preparation and finding ways to ensure authentic participation are essential to successful consensus workshops.

Preparation
Designing the workshop, both the focus question and the specific steps
The key to a successful workshop is designing a specific focus question that meets the need of

the group or organization. Think through all the factors that will influence the focus question and the success of the workshop. Start by naming the topic. Then list all those who have a stake in the results as well as the expected participants – and think through how all the stakeholders' perspectives can be held in the workshop. The rational aim clearly articulates the intended result that the group needs from the workshop, and the existential or experiential aim states how the group will be different at the end of their work together. The final area of concern is timing—both how long the results need to endure in the future, and how much time there is to do the workshop itself. All of this information shapes the focus question, which is an open-ended question that gets out many responses from each person that are elements of the necessary product or aim of the workshop. Figure 29 on page 171 is a template to help you think through the focus question.

After you have the focus question, plan the specific way you will do the workshop. If you lay out your plan using a landscape format, you can see all the steps in relation to the whole process, and keep track of how to allot enough time for each major stage of the process.

Think through how many small groups you will need, and how many cards each group should contribute so you end up with the optimal number of cards. While imagining the group you will be working with, write down how you will set the context, give brainstorming, clustering and naming instructions, and lead the resolve stage. Plan how much time you will spend on each stage of the process. Figure 30 in the appendix is a template to help you with your planning.

Preparation for delivery

Gather your materials, and then walk through the procedures step by step, either by yourself or with a colleague. If you discover parts of the process where you are uncertain about exactly what you will do or say, pay attention and work those out before the session.

Ensuring participation

It is important to intentionally set a context of respect at the beginning of a workshop, to encourage authentic participation and collaboration. These working assumptions set the groundwork for a successful consensus workshop:
- Working assumptions
- Everyone has wisdom.
- We need everyone's wisdom for the wisest result.
- There are no wrong answers.
- The whole is greater than the sum of its parts.
- Everyone will hear others and be heard.

You can find more detail to introduce these assumptions to a group in the appendix, page 169.

Allow enough time in the process for introverted people to have quiet time to think, and extroverted people to dialogue with others. If you have fewer than 30 people, do the small group work in pairs or threes so that everyone's ideas will get onto the cards. If you have more than 40 people, you may need the small groups to be larger, with a named small-group facilitator who will ensure everyone gets at least one idea on a card, and that the small group has the highest diversity of its ideas on cards.

Getting quality results

Each step of the workshop method carefully sets the stage for high quality results.

The *context* focuses the group on the topic. The context may begin with a presentation of background information, or a focused conversation on the topic that catalyzes thoughtful responses. Design the focus question carefully: it must be open-ended enough to elicit several different responses from each person, and these need to be elements that will create the needed product (the rational aim) when they are clustered together and named. Use the template to prepare the question, and then do a trial brainstorm with a colleague to test it before you start. It is in the context, also, where you share the working assumptions or ground rules, or create them with the group. An overview of the process you will use and the intended time for the steps also help the group relax and participate.

For the *brainstorming*, design specific sub-questions in advance to be comprehensive (and beyond bias). These questions will help people come up with a comprehensive and innovative list of concrete and specific answers to the focus question. For example, a mission statement workshop where the focus question is "Why are we in business?" might include sub-questions to trigger individual brainstorming like "Imagine a hundred years from now a history book is written that includes a chapter on your organization. What does it say?" or "Your child asks you why you work for your organization rather than another. What do you answer?"[47] The more diverse and comprehensive the brainstorm, the more insightful the larger ideas will be when they are clustered.

Often in the *clustering* stage, people struggle with the idea of gestalt or synthesis, and default to sorting ideas. Sharing a quick image of putting together a puzzle that doesn't have a box cover with the finished picture can help the group trust the process. It might go something like this: "Imagine for a minute that all your cards are pieces of a puzzle. Imagine you throw them into the middle of the table. What do you have? (a mess). OK, now imagine you take them all back and you are going to put together a picture puzzle – you don't have the box cover with the picture. What's the first thing you do when you put together a picture puzzle? (corners or borders) Then what do you do? (look for similar colours, or patterns, or lines that connect). Yes, and sometimes you'll see a crooked line starting to emerge and you think it is going to be a tree branch, but when you get a few more pieces you realize it's the side of a crooked roof or something else – the more pieces you have, the clearer the picture begins to be. What happens if you leave out a piece? (frustration, incomplete). Yes. The next stage of this process is much like putting together a picture puzzle for which we don't have the whole picture. We'll start with identifying 4 or 5 pairs of similar answers to the focus question, like putting the corners or borders on the puzzle. Then we'll look for other similar ideas, adding new pairs or adding ideas to the pairs we already have, until all the cards are up. We'll likely end up with somewhere between 5 and 9 clusters. Nothing will be left out. Then we'll name what we've come up with." This participatory story takes a couple of minutes and considerably reduces the group's struggle with clustering.

Use neutral symbols that don't carry embedded meaning to refer to each cluster (a smiley face

---

47 Staples, 2013, pp. 212-213

has embedded positivity: a circle is more neutral). Neutral symbols can help delay the urge to put meaning on a cluster until most cards are up – put a card with a symbol above or with each cluster as you work and insist that the group refer to the clusters using the symbols.

Also when clustering, you can ask questions that help people gestalt rather than sort—"Where does this card most helpfully illuminate a larger (or deeper) answer to the focus question?" or "Where is this card needed most?"—rather than "Where does this idea fit best?"

Gather cards in rounds so that you don't have more than 20 random (unclustered) cards on the wall at any time. Too many cards at once can overwhelm a group. In the third or next-to-last round, get up any cards that don't clearly fit, in order to broaden the gestalt before it solidifies. You can get these by asking the small groups to mark the cards that obviously overlap with a cluster already on the wall with that symbol, and send up any that they didn't mark. The last round, when everyone is exhausted, is then easy, because most cards will already fit easily in a cluster.

To *name* the clusters, refer back to the focus question. Each name will be one answer to the focus question. Using the focused conversation method to name clusters helps the group stay focused and explore the insight behind the cluster so that the results are more insightful. For example:

Objective: Read all the cards in the cluster out loud. (visual and auditory input)

Reflective: What words or phrases ON the cards jump out at you? (gut level clues to the cluster focus)

Interpretive: Explore the insight behind this cluster – what is the larger answer to the focus question that all these cards are pointing to? (exploring the meaning that has been created)

Decisional: Summarize the insight in a phrase that answers the focus question and write it on a card.

It is best to name each cluster one at a time with the whole group to articulate the group's consensus. This helps build support. It might be necessary to point out that no one has to agree with every card on the wall, and that the name cards are where the consensus is named. You might also find it helpful to say that "Consensus doesn't necessarily mean that everyone agrees. It means that everyone can support the result for the sake of moving forward."

The *resolve* stage is carefully designed to take the results on the wall and take the next step to make them into the needed results. Working toward a resolution usually starts with a focused conversation on the data on the wall, particularly the names of the clusters, which are where the consensus lies. There are many ways to then transform the clusters on the wall to useful results. For example, small groups can each take a cluster and write a sentence or paragraph that uses the language on the name card and the cards in the cluster as examples. They can be refined later if necessary, with care to ensure that the final wording still holds the wisdom of the group. Or the group can create a visual symbol or model that holds all the named elements of a solution or plan.

Addressing the existential aim

The existential aim is sometimes even more important than accomplishing the rational aim.

The working assumptions start to give the message that each person's idea is important wisdom, and will be a significant contribution to the group's wisdom and final result. When people feel heard, they have the possibility of trusting future work with their colleagues, even in situations of conflict or disagreement.

A consensus workshop can address feelings of isolation and marginalization as unique and diverse ideas help create innovative results. Small group work brings together people who don't often work together. Number off, or ask people to work with someone they don't know well. The activity of sharing ideas and including their diversity in small groups can build collaborative relationships that will benefit the group in the future.

When people ask each other questions of clarity first in small groups and then as cards come up on the wall, and then when they're asked in the clustering where a different idea is most needed rather than whether is a good or bad idea, respect for diversity begins to grow, and new connections are created within the group.

In many workshops, creating solutions together can diminish feelings of being overwhelmed and despair over obstacles. The creative results of a workshop can alter images of impossibility, and allow people to see options that they couldn't see alone. If a group feels ownership of the results, they are more likely to follow through to make things happen.

Examples of varied consensus workshop applications

The consensus workshop method is at the same time a very structured process and an infinitely variable tool that can be applied in a myriad of ways.

Edmonton public engagement

The City of Edmonton wanted to know from all its stakeholders what would make its public engagement process more effective. We facilitated about 25 2½ hour sessions using a consistent process with community people, staff and management, and then asked a representative group to draw all the results together. Each session included a focused conversation in small groups on people's previous experiences of public consultation, which opened the door for them to brainstorm answers to the question "What elements of effective public engagement are needed in the future in Edmonton?" and do a consensus workshop. The workshop was followed by a focused conversation to discover the importance of the elements, and simple brainstorm of principles to hold. A representative group took the 25 documents, which included more than 1000 different cards, and after they clustered the title cards from all the sessions, discerned and named the meta-patterns behind all the contributions. Every card was then documented to show where it added to the overall gestalt. The results are very powerful and the city is using them to design its public engagement processes.

Building scenarios of possible futures

A provincial department of education wanted to explore how they could approach distributed learning (including distance learning) in the future. They collected observations of trends from educators and other stakeholders across the province. They plotted these observations on the Social Process triangles[48], a comprehensive model of the economic, political, and cultural processes in any human grouping, to see where they coalesced to identify larger trends in society. They analyzed these trends to create four possible future scenarios. Then, a consensus workshop identified elements of a governance model for education that would support students in each of the scenarios. The nine core elements created were used to build possible models of governance.

Family planning session

Consensus isn't only for large or formal groups. When we were looking as a family to buy our first house, we did a simple consensus workshop with our family of four—one boy was 11, the other 17. We wrote the focus question, "What values do we want to hold in buying a house?" on a piece of paper and put it on the table in front of us. Then we used another piece of paper to capture the brainstorm. We then put symbols beside the items as we clustered them. The youngest son's "dog" idea clustered with my "garden" idea, and the underlying value became "access to a back yard." My husband's and my yearning to "live close to work" clustered with one son's ideas to "stay near school" and the other's "curb for skateboarding" to reveal the value of "an urban neighbourhood near our old apartment." We found a detached house with a backyard (instead of a condo) in an affordable neighbourhood not far from where we used to live.

Conclusion

The *consensus workshop method* is an elegantly simple way to gather a broad range of ideas and create larger insight. There are many different ways to lead a consensus workshop, but the approaches in alignment with the phenomenological method allow the group to synthesize new ideas based on the individual ideas they brought to the table.

Practical resources

For more information and detailed procedures for leading consensus workshops, please see *The Workshop Book* by Brian Stanfield, or try the ToP Group Facilitation Methods course[49].

---

48 Jenkins, 1997

49 http://www.ica-associates.ca/product/group-facilitation-methods/ or see http://www.ica-international.org/ica-worldwide to find training in other countries

7.
Participatory Strategic Planning

We are confronted with insurmountable opportunities.
　　　　　　　　—Sign in a W.L. Gore & Associates manufacturing plant in Flagstaff, Arizona

Success is not the result of spontaneous combustion. You must set yourself on fire.
　　　　　　　　　　　　　　　　　　　　　　　　　—Reggie Leach[50]

Regent Park Community Health Centre in Toronto chose to involve its board, staff, and members of their very diverse community in a participatory strategic planning process. First, they created a common vision of what they wanted the health centre to be like in five years. One insight was that they wanted local people in the community to be the doctors, nurses, social workers, community health workers, and administrators for their community. When they brainstormed the obstacles, they discerned that financial restraints and inconsistent family support were some of the underlying contradictions to students finishing high school, which prevented them from getting higher education and becoming professionals. Their strategies then included creating a detailed community-based support and accountability system for young people through high school. These supports would not only transform the graduation rate and enrollment in higher education, but also affect other determinants of health in the community, such as income levels and self-confidence. Action plans were made for all the strategies – the high school support program became "Pathways to Education." Further strategic planning helped them address more specific underlying contradictions in getting that program underway.

This groundbreaking program works because it was built by the people of a community who knew their problems and were convinced their vision was possible. Pathways to Education was so successful that it has been replicated in six provinces across Canada, currently involving 5,000 students, and increasing high school graduation rates by an average of 85 per cent. Over 73 per cent of grads go on to post-secondary education or training.

---

50 Reginald Joseph Leach is a retired Canadian hockey right winger who played for 13 seasons in the National Hockey League.

Background

The ToP *strategic planning method* grew out of the work of the Institute of Cultural Affairs in participatory community development. In the early 1970s, we expanded the work we had been doing in Fifth City, a neighbourhood on the west side of Chicago, with a plan to establish a community development project in every time zone around the world. It was necessary to evolve an authentic process that could be used in many cultures, so that the replication of the consultations could be done with consistency. We worked with the processes we had developed in the work with Fifth City to create a flexible set of procedures based on the phenomenological method. The consultation process included eliciting a vision, articulating the underlying contradictions, creating proposals to address the obstacles, developing a comprehensive tactical system to carry out the proposals, and creating programs to get the vision done. A regular recurring review process was also part of the process.

At about the same time, we developed a one-day event for local communities called a Community Forum or Town Meeting, which included inspiring talks about the "New World" and the "New People," as well as workshops on the contradictions in the community and strategies to deal with the contradictions, followed by a community celebration. Hundreds of these were held across North America in 1975 and 1976.

Some colleagues started to apply these methods to diverse companies and organizations to initiate ethical, respectful, participatory strategic planning. They created a two- to three-day retreat called LENS (Leadership Effectiveness and New Strategies), based on the same principles. This format often included workshops on Mission, Purpose, and Values along with the strategic planning focus. This work led to clarifying the method for use in all kinds of organizations, in the form now called *participatory strategic planning*.

Brief description

The basic ToP strategic planning methodology starts with articulating a shared *vision*. It then asks what is blocking that vision, reaching beneath the surface to identify the *underlying contradictions* that are keeping that vision from being realized. The next step is to create *strategies* that are aimed at the contradictions and could release the vision. The final step is creating action plans for *implementation*. Most often today, the *consensus workshop* method is used for the first three stages. Several tools have been developed by different groups for implementation planning.

ToP strategic planning, in all its variations, follows a natural human thinking process, as shown in Figure 7. Each of us has a latent vision of where we want to go that motivates and guides us. When we become conscious of our vision, we naturally begin to be aware of all that is preventing that vision from coming into being. When we articulate the root issues or contradictions beneath those blocks, we naturally begin to think of what we can do to address them, and then to come up with our next steps.

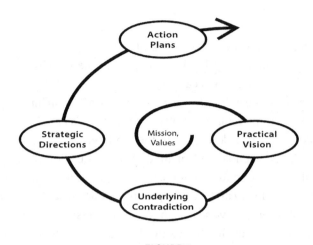

FIGURE 7

ToP strategic planning process showing the four steps

Purpose

The purpose of ToP participatory strategic planning is to guide a group to make plans that hold the tension between a long-range vision and practical day-to-day actions that people will actually do to make a difference. The method 1) inspires hope for the future (in the visioning exercise), 2) gently but firmly compels the group to acknowledge and take responsibility for the real situation (in the contradictions analysis), 3) creates catalytic strategies that build confidence that the group can influence their situation (in the strategies workshop), and then 4) builds concrete, practical actions that make that confidence practical and real (in the implementation or action planning step). As a result of the planning, the purpose is to encourage committed action on the plans followed by periodic participatory review that provides appreciation for what has been accomplished and continuous learning about what really works.

A deep purpose of this kind of strategic planning, is to release people from stories of "it can't be done," free people up from blame games, and catalyze them into taking responsibility for the future.

The four steps of the underlying process are also used as a problem-solving process as in What do we want to see? What is preventing this from happening? What can we do about it? What are our next steps?

The phenomenology behind participatory strategic planning

The ToP *strategic planning* process takes people through the four stages of perception, response, exploring meaning, and decision-making.

It begins with the *vision*, which provides the specific topic and a concrete beginning point. The process focuses on bringing to light the elements of the future that each person sees and operates from, consciously or unconsciously. In phenomenological terms it is the *thereness* – the objective reality that each of us is operating from.

The *response* is seen in the contradictions section that draws out each individual's response to the vision by looking at what is blocking that vision from becoming a reality. It is the gut-level reflective level response to the vision that emerged out of the previous session.

The *exploration* dynamic happens with the strategy session, which demands creativity and focus in dealing with the contradictions.

The *decision* dynamic occurs as the group takes the strategy and works through concrete implementation. This commitment becomes very tangible and real.

The four stages of the strategic planning process demonstrate *intentional focus*, *radical openness*, and *methods of inquiry* as in the focused conversation method and the consensus workshop method.

In addition, the *consensus workshop* used in each of the first three stages takes people through the same stages of perception, response, exploration and decision, which apply the phenomenological method. You start with describing what is observed through the external senses, expand consciousness to include the internal response, extrapolate patterns of meaning, and finally determine your response to the situation.

More on the application of phenomenology to strategic planning

Visioning is the act of bringing to awareness the hidden or unarticulated images that we already have about the future. Naming obstacles and underlying contradictions helps us "ground" our reality by looking for the underlying roots that keep surface level issues and problems going. Strategy creates practical momentum, hope and commitment as strategies are related primarily to addressing the underlying contradictions. Implementation and action plans make that commitment concrete and very real.

The whole process follows a natural thinking process where answers to each stage elicit the next focus question. After the vision is articulated, a response arises in each person – "yes, but…", seeing the blocks to the vision. When they name the underlying contradictions, people begin to think of what they can do to deal with them, giving rise to the strategies focus question, "What can we do to deal with the obstacles and realize our vision?" When they decide on strategies and align them in strategic directions, the questions of "Who is going to do this? What? Where? When?" arise and are answered through planning implementation and actions.

In basic ToP strategic planning, each of the first three stages applies the phenomenological pattern of gestalt, as in the *consensus workshop method* described on page 52.

Design patterns

The process requires four very different types of thinking:

The first is visionary thinking, which is motivational, future-oriented and flexible. It asks "What if?"

Next comes contradictional thinking, which is focused, deals with current reality, and acknowledges tensions. It asks "Why?"

Strategic thinking is directional, creative, and dynamic. It asks "Why not?"

Implementation plans evoke practical thinking, which is detailed, action-oriented and time-bound. This step asks "How to?"

Vision

During the vision stage, participants brainstorm their images of the future in answer to the focus question through individual silent brainstorming, which they then capture in writing or images. These images are present internally and may not have been conscious until you ask the question. This brainstorm makes the vision conscious and creates a visual product of the consensus that becomes the objective data upon which the next stages are based. For the silent brainstorming, you can lead a "guided daydreaming" (using a comprehensive screen such as the Social Process Triangles (see page 187) to help participants to stand in the future and see a comprehensive picture of what they have dreamed about.

When the group clusters the individual ideas and names the larger visions, a shared sense of the future emerges. The powerful process of digging deep to find individual visions, and then "gestalting" or clustering them to create shared vision energizes the group. The vision covers both real needs and felt needs. It must go beyond tame and fairly predictable ideas to include items that provoke a few Wow!s. At the same time the vision should not become so abstract that it is not tied to reality. The process of creating a shared vision is at least as important as the final strategic plan, as this is where participants begin to see that they are aligned and that there is consensus in what they want.

Contradictions

The contradictions process is the most challenging part of strategic planning, but it is key to effective strategic thinking. The brainstorm begins with the vision, the objective part of the process, and then explores the blocks or obstacles that keep the vision from happening. The clustering intuitively explores the contradictions underlying these blocks, and the naming of the clusters is where a group can experience a breakthrough.

A contradiction lies in that gap that any sensible person knows about—the gap between one's intention for a situation and what actually comes to be. In Western philosophy, Hegel came closest to describing what a contradiction is. His philosophy was based upon thesis and antithesis, out of which emerges a synthesis. Out of the tension of a thrust and a counter-thrust comes the "not yet." T.S. Eliot said it best: "Between the idea and the reality falls the Shadow."[51] The contradiction is the

---

51 Eliot,1967

shadow that intervenes between what we want to do and getting it done. The contradiction is what-ever says NO to the practical vision—contradicting and negating it. You know you have named a contradiction when you are driven to write proposals or create strategies. Acknowledging the reality of the situation and taking the time to see the roots beneath our surface irritations, issues and com-plaints is not easy.

The focus question is "What is blocking our vision?" The brainstorm step allows people to describe and acknowledge rather than ignore, fear or romanticize obstacles. Obstacles include both external deterrents to the vision as well as internal irritants and frustrations. When you intuitively cluster all these blocks by underlying obstacle in clumps around a centre point, people can discern patterns of relationships that reveal hidden insights. (See the "polar gestalt" on page 56.) The clus-tering process is important to help the group to gently arrive at the underlying roots they contribute to that sustain the problematic situation. Naming the contradiction examines the relationships and gives a name to the deeper sociological condition that we all participate in, which both blocks our vision and provides a doorway to the future. Name each contradiction descriptively.

This method reaches beneath anxiety, cynicism, bitching and romanticism to articulate real patterns that we participate in. Discerned contradictions transform despair to hope, when we acknowledge that we are a part of the problem and therefore can do something about it. At the resolution stage of the contradictions process, pick one or more of the named contradictions and ask, "If we deal with this contradiction, which elements of our vision will it release?" Most often, addressing any one contradic-tion will release more than one element of the vision. It is helpful to have each person share an action they can take to address any one of the obstacles before they leave an obstacles workshop, to move the group's thinking toward what they can do rather than to fall back into hopelessness.

Strategies

Brainstorming strategies completes the shift from acknowledging the reality of the situation to generating creative and practical responses, and is often the most challenging part of the strategies workshop. When the contradictions process has been done thoroughly, strategies come more eas-ily. The focus question is "What *can we do* to deal with the obstacles *and* realize our vision?" The emphasis is on *can* (possible, not *ought*), *we* (the people in the room), *do* (actions), and *and* (accom-plishing both jobs).

To ensure comprehensiveness, ask each participant to brainstorm at least one or two different actions to deal with each one of the obstacles, and then to choose some concrete actions that are really creative as well as some that are more conserving or take less energy. Cluster these brain-stormed actions by "actions that can be done together to create momentum," creating practical strategies. You can then cluster the strategies again at a higher level to show their alignment in strategic directions. At the resolve stage of the workshop, it is helpful for each person to write their name on the strategy or strategies they are committed to work on. The experience of the group at the end of the strategies workshop is excitement, momentum and commitment, with a bit of awe as awareness of responsibility kicks in.

Implementation

If you stop a strategic planning process at articulating strategies, the strategic plans stay on the shelf, because they don't address the next set of human questions that arise: Who is going to do this? When? Where? What will it cost?

The *rational aim* of implementation and action plans is to have concrete, doable, yet inspiring plans that will move the strategies forward, address the obstacles, and realize the vision. The *existential or experiential aim* is for people to be inspired, commit to moving forward together, and take responsibility for the actions. There are some variations in how this stage of the process is accomplished, as described in the next section, but the overall objectives are the same.

Of course, after you have the plan, the next stages are actually carrying out the actions, and periodic review and re-planning. These stages provide regular reality checks, accountability and re-planning using lessons learned from the implementation. The openness that is built into the process of regular review of short-term action plans, celebrating both accomplishments and setbacks and using the learning from the review to make new plans, is a phenomenological process in that it activates consciousness of the current situation and our relationship to it, and evokes an intentional response.

Design pattern variations

Beginning the process

For effective strategic planning, preparation is essential before the four stages described above. Each step contributes to the clarity of focus of the process and helps keep participants engaged.

Preparing for strategic planning

1) Assessing the internal and external reasons for strategic planning. Sometimes an external force such as a funder demands a strategic plan, as happened to a number of government-supported agencies in the late 1980s when funding was only given when a strategic plan was in place. If the group can see the opportunity that demand can bring, planning can be successful. Internal reasons could be to make a cultural change, or to become more cost-effective, or to grow successfully. Asking the client "Why do you want to do strategic planning?" helps assess the readiness of the group. Also ask "How will you use the plan?" to clarify their real intent, which isn't always initially stated.

2) Clarifying the planning objectives—expectations, results, scope, group. Often every person in an organization that asks for a strategic plan has a different idea of what they expect to accomplish, what scope the process will cover, what the results should be, and who should be involved. Spending time discussing this with the sponsor and other key people will set a successful path for the planning session.

3) Establishing the planning roles and guidelines—participation, steering committee, leadership, facilitator. It is usually helpful if more people than the sponsor are involved in steering or leading from the organization as they will have different perspectives to inform the process. Encouraging participation from as many stakeholder groups as possible in the planning process will strengthen the plans and increase commitment and support in the end.

4) Designing the planning process—focus question, methods, time. An overall focus question agreed upon by the steering group or leadership will keep things on track throughout the process. This is not the same as a focus question for a workshop; rather, it defines the parameters of the planning at a high level, and is an overarching question that the whole process will answer. For example, an overall focus question might be "What does our focus need to be in the next few years to make us a strong, viable organization that is accomplishing our mission?" A focus question for the vision workshop in this example would be "What do we want the organization to look like in 5 years?"

To do the planning process in its classic form with three workshops plus action planning requires at least four sessions or two days. If the sessions need to be broken up, it is better to break after the vision session and again after strategies, rather than after contradictions. The struggle to acknowledge and take responsibility for the contradictions can intensify and cause despair unless there is an immediate turn to strategies. A vision can stand on its own for a while, and action plans are sometimes better done after a break of a few days in order to give time to create the implementing teams.

If fewer than two days can be set aside for planning, there are some ways to shorten the steps and still maintain most of the process. It is not wise to do more than three of the stages in one day, as it takes an immense mental effort to shift thinking styles from visionary to contradictional to strategic thinking, and people can become exhausted from that intensity.

Developing the planning context

1) Analyzing the external environment—stakeholders and constituents, competitors and collaborators, events, trends, opportunities and threats. The ToP tool called *frameworking* is a good tool to analyze the stakeholders of a project (see Figure 31 on page 173). You can also do a *consensus workshop* to identify potential competitors and collaborators. You can use either of these tools with a planning team to help ensure that participants represent a wide range of perspectives to enrich the results.

A broad journey wall that includes external events in the world and the region or field can help identify external trends, opportunities and threats that will impact the organization's plans (see pages 110-119). Or you can lead a workshop on threats and another on opportunities. The information from threats will inform the obstacles, and that from opportunities will inform vision and strategies.

2) Analyzing the internal environment—history, accomplishments and setbacks, resources, strengths and weaknesses. Very often doing a journey wall helps clarify the milieu and provide a broader context before facilitating their vision. Deeply understanding the whole of the past provides a solid stance in the present, which allows a real visioning of the future. The journey wall is best done for a broad time frame, often the history of the organization or some other time period that is meaningful to the organization. Try to include a stream of world events, one of regional or professional events, and a stream of organizational events. These broader streams set the stage for reflecting on trends that are useful for thinking about the future. (See Chapter 9 about the *journey wall* method (also called the *wall of wonder*), starting on page 103.)

A broad journey wall of a significant period as mentioned in analyzing the external environment, followed by a focused conversation, will bring out substantial data about the internal environment as well, including accomplishments and setbacks, and strengths and weaknesses of the internal environment. An internal survey or conversation can also bring out strengths, which will inform strategies, and weaknesses, which will inform contradictions.

3) Clarifying the mandates and mission–basic mandate, purpose, reason for being. Sometimes mandates and mission can be pictured as the centre around which the strategic planning spiral moves. A purpose or mission workshop and values brainstorm are often helpful before starting a strategic planning process–if an organization doesn't know why it exists or what values it stands for, it is very hard to project the future they want. Again, you can use the consensus workshop method. For step-by-step procedures, see *Winning Through Participation* by Laura Spencer[52] and also *Transformational Strategy*, by Bill Staples[53].

If the group already has a strong mission statement that still applies, you can begin with a focused conversation on the mission statement that "grounds" each phrase: "When we see this part of our mission being acted out in real life, what do we see?" The participation in creating or recreating the mission often motivates the group more than the final result.

4) Making the primary values–guiding principles, basic ethics, and operating patterns objective. Often an organization has already articulated its values, but they can become abstract, meaningless phrases devoid of life. If so, lead a grounding conversation—"What does it look like when we hold each of these in our everyday work and life?" If the group has not stated its values, it is wise to do a consensus workshop to create the values and principles before the strategic planning, keeping the language as clear and concise as possible. The articulation of values guides the focus of the strategic planning process, particularly the vision.

Facilitating the Creation of Strategies

At this point, you move into the four stages of the spiral, as described above and shown in Figure 8:
1. Stating the vision of the future
2. Identifying the underlying contradictions
3. Creating the strategic directions
4. Designing the implementation scheme

Timing and pacing
The classic design for the strategic planning process takes a half day (three to four hours) for each of the four stages of the process, generally over two consecutive days; or an afternoon, a full day, and the next morning.

It is better not to have a long break between obstacles and strategies; the breakthrough from acknowledging the underlying contradictions to evolving creative strategies to deal with them often happens just as the strategy brainstorm begins. Letting people go at the end of contradictions may leave them in unresolved despair.

---

52 Spencer, 1989
53 Staples, 2012

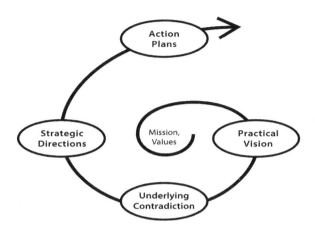

FIGURE 7

ToP strategic planning process showing the four steps

It is important for the group to acknowledge and celebrate their past in order to stand grounded in the present and be able to envision the future. Be sure to build in enough time to do an journey wall or a conversation on their accomplishments and setbacks before starting the vision workshop.

Sometimes a client insists that they only have one day to create a strategic plan. This is not wise, because shifting among the different kinds of thinking is exhausting, and there is not enough time to have important conversations at each stage. If there is no other option, the vision, obstacles, and strategies can be done in an eight- to nine-hour session, but it will feel long. Action plans will have to be done at another time or by the small groups who will implement them.

If the visioning section is left out, the obstacles begin with complaints about anything and may in fact have little or nothing to do with what is blocking the organization from achieving its vision. Participants will struggle with the difficult topic and resist the method. If obstacles are left out, the strategies are often ungrounded, without taking the realities into consideration. As one client said, "Now I see why my strategies have never worked—they are aimed directly at the vision, and the obstacles get in the way and prevent success!"

It is possible to do an obstacles conversation instead of a workshop if time is limited and there is a general feeling that the obstacles are not overwhelming. An example of an obstacles conversation can be found on page 176.

Preparation for delivery

As in the workshop method, make sure you take time to write your procedures for each workshop and walk through them in detail beforehand, imagining the group you are working with to iron out any gaps in the process. You may have to adapt the procedures as you work with the group, but you will have a very good sense of what you are adjusting from and the consequences of any changes.

Workshop	Context	Brainstorm	Chart	Launch	Resolve
Overview of Sections	Overview of Implementation Workshop to prepare group for making strategic decisions about what needs to be accomplished in Year One.	**One Year Accomplishments** Brainstorm of one year accomplishments for each strategic direction: State with the current reality, then success indicators, then critical accomplishments for each strategy for the year. This is best done by the entire group (see variations based on size/time below).	**Quarterly Calendar** One Year Accomplishments are placed on a quarterly calendar and assignments are made to teams or individuals.	**90 Day Plans** 90 Day Plans are developed for first quarter accomplishments. This can be done for all the accomplishments for teams or for one or two by the whole group.	Group determines 90 Day Priorities by identifying the top 6, reflecting or clarifying the values, and placing them on a wedge or other arrangement as a focusing launch symbol.
Flip Charts and Cue Cards What are Cue Cards?	Write Workshop Question on flip chart. What will be our specific measurable accomplishments for the first year? Optional: Create an overview flip chart with the following 4 sections	Create one flip chart for each strategic direction SD: CR Accomp. Success Indicator 1. 2. 3. 4. 5. 6. 7. Scribe writes accomplish-ments on half sheets (colour-coded by SD)	Layout for wall. Use coloured half sheets for quarters. Q1 Q2 Q3 Q4 ⇑ ⇑ ⇑	1 flip chart for each of the 8 to 10 Q accomplishments plus 8.5 x 11 work and documentation sheets. **90 Day Plan** SD: Accomp.:	Flip chart for 90 Day Priorities
Other Materials		• Have SD boxes in clear view • Half sheets • 2 sets of markers in same 3-4 colours (or 3-4 colours of half sheets)	• Coloured half sheets for quarter title cards and strategic direction arrows • Accomplishments written on half sheets • Large post-its (if assigning individuals)	• 8.5 x 11 90 Day Plans work and report sheets (10 to 12)	
Option for Large Group		Do all SDs simultaneously forming teams for each direction with a designated facilitator and scribe for each group.	Teams phase their accomplishments and place on calendar. Plan for sufficient report time and modifying input from whole group.	No change.	No change.
Option for Limited Time		Do SDs simultaneously as above.	Same, but ensure sufficient report time and input opportunity from total group.	Do one or two sample plans as a group as examples and encourage assigned groups to do the rest as soon as possible.	Omit.

FIGURE 9

A visual overview of the U.S. implementation process

Planning the Implementation

The implementation stage is how strategic planning makes a difference. This is where things happen. You need an overall implementation scheme to provide a comprehensive plan for how actions will be carried out.

Which strategies will be worked on first, or will the group work on each strategy simultaneously? If possible, it is best to do some small steps on each of them simultaneously, so that the obstacles are addressed from more than one direction at a time. Sometimes it is important to focus on one strategy first to open the door for work on others.

Who will work on each one? Rather than assigning strategies to individuals, teamwork is more effective. If the organization is small, perhaps a team can work together on a strategic direction rather than a single strategy.

Implementation depends on identifying an overall timeline for the actions. Generally, a three- to six-month timeframe works well to increase momentum and allow for timely review and re-planning as needed.

Next, assignments are made to work on action plans, with the assumption that those who plan the action are the primary people who will do the actions. This mitigates making abstract or un-doable plans, because people can see what they are committing themselves to.

In practice, two main approaches to the implementation process have been developed by ToP colleagues in the United States and Canada. For simplicity, we'll call them the American and Canadian approaches, but they're not really tied to place.

The American approach to the implementation workshop

This introduction is from the U.S. training manual for the Participatory Strategic Planning course[54]:

> In this workshop, the group moves from analyzing and thinking about all the creative things that could be done to concrete decisions about what will be done. The actions that are agreed upon have the power to beckon the commitment of those who design them and to catalytically influence the environment and relationships in which they are implemented. Not everything thought of can be done at once. Therefore, focusing and prioritizing are needed in each strategy.

The implementation workshop has three major parts: In the first part, the group determines its major accomplishments for the first year for each strategic direction. The accomplishments are specific and concrete. The actions have an ending point, so they can be accomplished within a specific time period rather than be ongoing activities, and they are measurable in that you know if you did them or not.

In the second part of the workshop, participants create a quarterly calendar that establishes by when each accomplishment will be completed. The calendar provides a clear picture of all that the group is proposing and allows for reflection on its "do-ability" and timing. Often at this point, it is

---

54 http://ica-usa.org/top-courses/planning-multi.htm

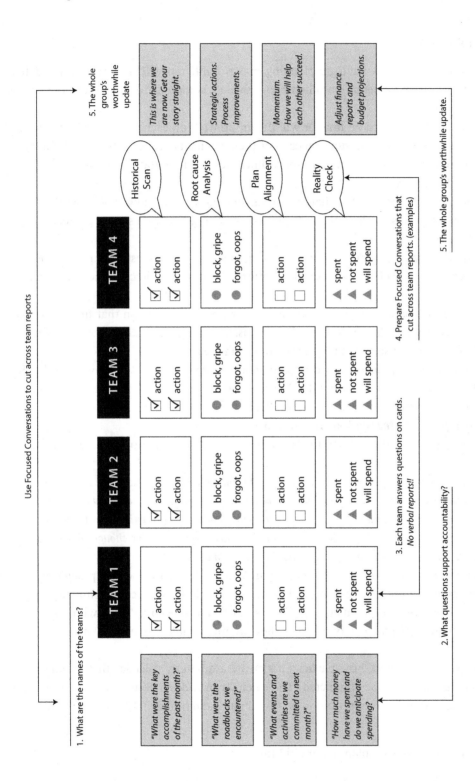

FIGURE 10

Team report and reflection matrix

also determined who will be responsible for each accomplishment, so it is important that those who are going to be involved in the implementation of the plan participate in this workshop.

In the third part, if time permits, the group creates 90-day activity plans for each accomplishment for the first quarter. In this process, resources are aligned, roles and responsibilities are assigned, and team trust and support begin to develop. This process is summarized in Figure 9.

The implementation plan creates action and in turn generates more action towards the intended outcome. It adds to, subtracts from, and alters situations and relationships. It brings into reality strategies that, when evaluated, provide the means of learning for a group or an organization. Integral to this process is the assumption that there will be quarterly "re-maneuvering" sessions to evaluate the past 90 days and to make any necessary adjustments to the plan for the next 90 days. Also implied is that a new 12-month plan will need to be created at the end of year one and, if the strategic directions remain on target, at the end of year two and possibly, year three.

The Canadian action planning process

In Canada, we use an elaboration of the action planning process described in Chapter 8 (starting on page 96). It is a microcosm of the strategic planning process, as it identifies possible accomplishments for a short-term period (a visioning activity), identifies strengths, weaknesses, benefits and dangers (becoming clear on current reality), and chooses a concrete measurable accomplishment to accomplish by a specific time. The group then brainstorms the actions needed to make this accomplishment happen, and sequences them on a timeline. A slogan or symbol is created to turn these actions into an action campaign. Then the people who are committed to the actions are named and the costs are projected. This is usually done in small groups with a detailed workbook to guide each step. This process keeps the planning grounded in reality at each step. At a final plenary each strategy team shares their measureable accomplishment, actions on the timeline, symbol or slogan, team members, and projected cost. This sharing allows for the coordination of the whole action plan, and sets a time to review the whole. For more detail, see Chapter 8, Action Planning, starting on page 88 and also the templates in the appendix starting on page 181.

Turning the plans into reality

Implementing the plan

However the plans are created, the rubber hits the road when it comes to implementation. As people implement the plans, some parts will be easily accomplished, and others will be more difficult. The environment around the activities will change and make some accomplishments impossible. Some movement on the strategies will happen completely independent of the plans.

Monitoring the action and evaluating the results

Tracking action, action reviews, breakthroughs and gaps, learnings, and current position become important to keep momentum going. Brief weekly or monthly "check signals" or action review meetings are helpful to keep everyone on track and support those who are struggling. At slightly longer intervals, a more thorough participatory review and reflection helps to clarify what has been accomplished whether it was planned or not, and identifies new contradictions that have arisen.

Refocusing the plans

Re-planning starts from the new current situation. It is difficult to follow a linear action plan for more than six months, as history changes around us at an ever faster pace. Review and re-planning of the action plans is best done every six months, reviewing and updating strategies every year or two, and the entire strategic planning process every three to five years.

Review and refocusing the plans

Review of action plans is best done every three to six months to celebrate successes and also to identify emerging challenges and allow for changes in direction. For this periodic review, several good tools are available. One is a short-term journey wall, which covers the action planning period. Events, accomplishments, setbacks, and other events that have happened are brainstormed and put on a timeline on the wall. (See page 119.) This scan becomes the objective data that leads to thinking through what the current situation is and what the group has learned about planning and action so that these insights can be applied to further action planning.

John Miller developed a matrix for reflecting on and re-planning where each team can quickly summarize their accomplishments, roadblocks, future commitments and money and put them on the wall. Then they have a focused conversation about each of these topics: the accomplishments of the whole group, the roadblocks the whole group has faced, and so on. This matrix, as seen in Figure 10, provides a very quick way to update everyone, think deeply, and then apply these learnings in planning the next action stage.

Ensuring participation

Ambiance

The ideal room for strategic planning has several blank flat walls on which you can stick cards, so that you can leave the results of each workshop up to prompt the brainstorm for the next workshop. The group should be seated so they can see and hear each other and the working wall. If you have more than 20 people, you may want to set up tables in a half-circle or horseshoe shape, with people seated around the back of the tables so they can see the front wall. Light on the working wall is important so that people can read the cards.

Setting the context

Use the working assumptions or ground rules on page 169 to set the context for respectful participation.

Ways to engage people

If far-flung stakeholders need to be engaged but cannot physically come to the group session, it is possible to do an electronic or paper survey that gives the context, then asks each of the focus questions in order, leaving room for individual responses to each question. In the face-to-face session, these ideas can then be distributed among the small groups in the room to be transferred on to cards, as if they are invisible members of the small group. The challenge is that the data has to be verbatim, since the writer is not present to explain or clarify the meaning of the words they wrote.

If there are hundreds of people who need to be engaged, it is useful to do small "focus group" workshops with small groups in different locations and times so that they can contribute in person. Each session will take at least three hours, as you do quick vision, obstacles, and strategies workshops. Each result is documented and compiled with the others. Then a representative of each group comes to a "plenary" session to pull the results together, using the original cards from the focus groups. For each of the three workshops, first the group clusters the "name" cards from each focus group and names the "meta-clusters," which are a higher level of gestalt formed from the small group names. Then the individual data cards are sorted within the meta-clusters, and the common themes or elements within each meta-cluster are named. In this way, each person can track how their particular idea contributes to the end result.

Achieving high quality results

A very important element in ensuring the best possible results is to provide enough time for each of the stages.

Participants need to be grounded in the current reality so they are able to create a practical vision. The visioning brainstorm benefits from a comprehensive "daydreaming" exercise that takes time but allows access to the deep hopes and dreams of each participant. (See pages 174-175.)

Obstacles can be clustered intuitively to reveal contradictions, but time is needed for the deep conversation required to explore and name the underlying contradictions. If the process is hurried along, you might not get to ownership of the contradictions and real breakthroughs.

Strategy brainstorming that is done too quickly can generate vague or cookie-cutter actions such as "just do it" or "communication" which do not lead to practical, catalytic strategies that can make a difference.

Quick action planning assignments that cut across the team structures in an organization, or quick lists of actions that don't consider the work people are already doing will not be productive.

For high quality results, most groups need at least two to three hours for a vision workshop; at least three hours for an obstacles workshop; a minimum of two hours for a strategies workshop; and at least four hours for action planning, including an introduction to the workbook, creating the specific plans, and a plenary session to coordinate and finesse the overall action plan. Leaving at least overnight but not more than a week between the strategies workshop and action planning is wise, so people have a chance to think through the action planning teams and how they work with the organization's structure.

Addressing the existential aim

ToP strategic planning acknowledges the journey of individuals and groups and helps them strategically plan directions for the future. In the visioning exercise, deep and sometimes invisible personal hopes and dreams are accessed and synthesized with those of other participants to create a common vision that is exciting and motivating. Each person senses themselves as a part of a hopeful larger vision and sees that they are not alone. The underlying contradictions workshop moves each person and the group gently from paralysis and blame for problems to an understanding of how each person participates in the underlying contradiction and therefore has the power to do something about it. This can be a profound existential shift that allows a "yes!" to the situation as it is, enabling them to affect it. The strategies workshop creates a sense that when we work together to address the contradictions, we can make a difference–a practical and grounded sense of hope. The action planning process asks people to plan for what they themselves will do, therefore creating a sense of responsibility and possibility for making the future happen.

A major existential aim of the strategic planning process is a realistic, grounded sense of hope and responsibility for the future.

Comparison with other strategic planning methods

"Traditional" strategic planning

Traditional strategic planning generally is an analytical and quite linear process which includes diagnosing the current situation, setting goals, determining the actions to achieve the goals, and implementing the actions. Often it is the responsibility of senior leadership. ToP strategic planning is more like the strategic thinking process that Henry Mintzberg described in *The Rise and Fall of Strategic Planning*[55] than strategic planning. There are two major differences from linear planning: In the ToP process, obstacles are a critical stage between vision and strategy. This approach was created from observing the steps people go through when they effectively solve problems and synthesizing the process. The consequence is to make the strategies more effective and grounded. In addition, ToP strategic planning is not linear, but iterative. Review, reflection and re-planning happen after every stage of implementation as an intentional part of the process, and this iterative nature allows both mid-course corrections and immediate implementation of learning as the planning is implemented. This spiral is not flat, but three-dimensional, as the review at the end of the arrow leads to visioning again at a higher level of development.

Emphasis on participation

Another uniqueness of ToP strategic planning is its strong participatory bias. Many clients ask for an expert outside consultant to analyze the situation and create a strategic plan for the organization. ToP strategic planning assumes that the people inside the organization, including front-line people as well as management and sometimes the clients, have the wisdom to think strategically together to come up with a winning plan. Also, it assumes that people are more likely to implement what they themselves have planned to do.

SWOT analysis

If you are familiar with SWOT analysis (strengths, weaknesses, opportunities and threats)[56], you may have noticed that the four elements of this method are included in steps one and two of

---

55 Mintzberg, 1994

56 https://en.wikipedia.org/wiki/SWOT_analysis or https://www.sri.com/sites/default/files/brochures/dec-05.pdf, page 7.

developing the planning context in the design section above. The articulation of internal strengths and external opportunities gives important information for the vision and strategic direction workshops, and the internal weaknesses and external threats are useful information for brainstorming obstacles. In itself, doing a SWOT analysis is not a complete strategic plan, but it gathers useful information. If you use a SWOT analysis, it is helpful for the mood of a group to work through threats before opportunities, so that the group ends on a positive note.

Examples of strategic planning applications

A simple, small, uncontroversial situation

A provincial government made the existence of a strategic plan mandatory for funding of service organizations. An organization that served developmentally challenged clients decided that they needed to invest two days in creating a strategic plan. They included staff, administration, parents, and a few clients in the weekend sessions. They used the classic format: a vision workshop followed by an obstacles workshop on Saturday and a strategies workshop and action planning process on Sunday. Their strategic plan was accepted by the province. Their experience was so positive that they recommended it to other similar organizations. Some of these organizations followed up with a six-month action planning review, celebrating their accomplishments, learning about how best to plan, and making new plans.

A large, complex, important and contentious situation

The Cree School Board in northern Quebec wanted to do a comprehensive strategic plan that engaged parents, students, teachers, and administration. The first focus group that created vision, obstacles and strategies was with the leadership team of the school board. They then decided to do a focus group session in every community school over a four-month period and draw together the results. The school committee in each of the nine communities set up their local event and invited local people. The attendance ranged from 20 to 120 people, and the cards were generated in Cree, French and English. A local school person documented each session as it happened, and the local school got a copy of their verbatim results right after the session. The leadership, which represented all the communities, then gathered for two days in a plenary session to create the overall vision, obstacles and strategic directions. Each school then chose one or more strategies and did their own action plan, using a common template. Five years later the school board was still operating out of the consensus on their strategic plan, and proud of their accomplishments.

Doing an obstacles conversation instead of a workshop

A small university department had a new dean who believed strongly in participation, and was replacing a more dictatorial dean. They could only carve out a day for a strategic plan. The dean had experienced the process with another organization, and knew the potential impact of cutting corners because of time, but said that the depth of the product was not as important as the team-building and trust-building across faculty members that would happen during the process. So they started at 8 AM with vision, then did an obstacles conversation, then spent the most time on strategies for moving forward. The team created a new sense of collaboration with each other and the dean, which had long-term results for the productivity of their work.

How the thinking process happens even when the process is not explicit

The City of Edmonton did an extensive consultation to define what people wanted to see in effective public engagement. This was not articulated as a visioning process, but they did ask what people wanted to see. As the plenary process articulating the elements was wrapping up, people began to ask, "Why don't we already do this?" So the city did another stage in the process to discern the blocks and the underlying contradictions and then strategies to address them. Although the process was not presented as strategic planning, the underlying human thinking process was triggered and used as a pattern to design the next stages of the consultation process.

Doing a journey wall before creating the vision

The Yellowknives Dene First Nation in the North Slave Region of the Northwest Territories chose to do their first strategic planning as a retreat at Enodah, on their traditional land. The session was held with a cross-section of the community in the cook tent, which was made of a wood 2x4 structure covered by canvas walls. They asked to do a 200-year journey wall, since they had never pulled together and documented their own history. Flipchart pages were strung up on a clothesline in front of a bearskin and a wolfskin on the wall, and masking tape with the sticky side out was used to hold small cards with events. Cards were generated by people of all ages in both Dogrib and English. At the end of the journey wall, with all the sections named, a young woman read back the whole scan in Dogrib. At this point, the elders spoke up and said "Yes, this is our story. Now we will leave it to the young people to plan the future, as they will be living it and making it happen." The young people then completed the vision, obstacles, strategies and catalytic action plans, while the elders smoked meat and sewed nearby. The documented journey wall was enlarged and displayed on the wall of the community centre in Ndilo. Several years later, community leaders updated the strategic plan during a combination hunting and strategic planning retreat on another part of their traditional land.

Purpose and values workshops

Generally, if an organization needs to clarify its purpose and values, it is best to do that first, before starting the strategic planning process so that the organizational purpose sets a context for vision. However, the IT department of a school system insisted on doing their strategic plan first because the system had a mission statement. When they identified strategies, they realized they needed a strategy to create a specific mission and purpose for their department. So they held a one-day retreat to create a mission. They used the procedures for a mission workshop that you can find in the book *Transformational Strategy*[57]. At the resolution stage of the workshop on mission, they broke into three groups. One wrote a mission statement in prose from the mission elements. A second created a visual logo for the department, using the elements as the starting point. A third group created a song from the elements. The song was silly, and made the whole team laugh and come together as they tried to sing it together. Several months later, a visit to their department showed that a new sense of camaraderie had transformed the department and the strategies were making a difference.

---

57 Staples, 2012, pages 211-217

Online strategic planning elements

One way to use the first three steps in the process asynchronously online is to ask the focus question for each step in a survey or on a website or discussion forum, or even in Twitter. You can gather the answers for a small representative group to cluster and name, and then send them back to participants for their editing. In Twitter, you can use a hashtag to gather the ideas, and someone can look for patterns in the answers and post them with the hashtag.

The first three stages can also be facilitated synchronously online, using a desktop sharing program with a mindmap program, or a platform that allows writing "sticky notes" and moving them to cluster them (such as Stormboard or Spilter), or a platform with a virtual whiteboard such as Blackboard Collaborate where participants can put moveable text boxes.

Online work on implementation planning requires a platform that can allow participants to fill in the action planning template together.

Impact of this method

The impact of ToP strategic planning can range from simple gratitude for a clear consensus on a plan to major cultural transformation in an organization.

Establishing a culture of participation

A number of groups have used the process when a new director or team leader with an understanding of participation replaced a top-down, hierarchical boss. The act of asking people for their visions and having them bring them together in larger patterns, then struggling together to name the deep contradictions and finally commit to practical strategies gives a signal to the group that they are going to be respected and appreciated. In organizations that have used this approach, follow-up sessions have indicated that the culture of fear begins to dissipate and employees become more positive and motivated.

For example, one community organization was deeply divided. Its activities were based on the activist philosophy of "fighting the oppressor on behalf of the oppressed." In the naming of the underlying contradictions suddenly one participant, looking at the biggest cluster, said, "It's the us-and-them mindset that we are based on–we've turned it inward and it is killing us!" The body language of everyone in the group showed that the message hit home, but it was extremely difficult to face the fact that their cherished belief also catalyzed the behaviours that were destroying them. They tried to escape the challenge, but finally named it. A year later they told another facilitator that that was a turning point, (even though they hadn't liked the facilitator for guiding them to that insight), that they had addressed this contradiction and the organization had become much more stable.

Building an effective coalition

Another client was a diverse regional group of health organizations that wanted to form an effective coalition. There were many overlaps in mandates and turf among the organizations, and they wanted to create a coherent strategy to effectively use their resources to address health needs in the region. The strategic planning process allowed all the voices to be heard, and they successfully created a coalition.

Catalyzing inclusion

One organization provided services for developmentally challenged people. They decided to have some of their clients participate in the strategic planning process, although they didn't really believe that they could participate in an intellectual process. One "labeled" young man, Jacques, during the vision brainstorming, said to the facilitator, "Tree! Forest! Fall down, die! Bring workshop, make furniture! You hear? You hear?" The facilitator listened through the metaphor and realized that he meant that people who are considered dead and useless would be brought into the community and made a useful part of it. He drew his tree on a card and his small group wrote a few words on the card to explain it. That idea clustered with the other ideas that pointed to an integrated community, and provided richness. In the obstacles workshop clustering, when he heard the cards being read out loud as they were put on the wall, he suddenly jumped up and shouted "Ring, ring, ring! You hear? You hear?" Someone on the other side of the room responded, "You mean the fire drill we had last week?" Jacques cried out "You hear! Ring, ring, go out, cold, door closed, can't get in!" What Jacques meant was that people were excluded from the real life of the community. He drew a fire bell on a card and the card clustered with others that pointed to underlying barriers that prevented inclusion in the community. Then the whole group went on to create the strategies and action plans.

Eight years later, this story had become a teaching story for inclusion of stakeholders in planning, and was used in a training session involving some of the same people in that community. A woman came up to the trainer and said, "That event was a real turning point in our organization. Before that time, we created programs and slotted our clients into them. Because of Jacques' participation, we realized that our clients knew what they wanted in their lives. Now (and it took us five years to fully make the change) we sit down with our clients first and find out what they want, and then find ways to support them. We still have some of the same programs, but we come at it from a totally different perspective. It was that strategic planning and Jacques' participation that enabled us to make this major shift in our organization."

Catalyzing effective local initiatives

In the 1970s, ICA used the participatory strategic planning process with villages and inner city communities across the world to do participatory community development. In Bayad, Egypt, an ancient farming village from the time of the Pharoahs across the Nile River from Beni Suef, for example, villagers and "experts" from Egypt and around the world came together to do strategic planning. The diverse perspectives of residents and people who had expertise in various fields expanded everyone's perspectives. One overwhelming vision of the community was to have clean water that did not carry bilharzia and other diseases, because they got their water directly from the Nile or from a narrow canal along the village boundary. Another was to get adequate educational opportunities for their children.

Each step in the strategic planning process took a full day, as facilitators and translators gathered brainstorming in kitchens across the community in order to include the voices of women who did not come out to public meetings. The brainstorms were written in Arabic and English on portable blackboards, and those in the face-to-face sessions clustered and named them on the blackboards. As a result of the planning process, within 6 months a hand-dug well provided clean water to the community, and a preschool was founded with local women teachers, among other changes. Forty years later, Bayad has a full water system with clean drinking water and sanitation, and local women still run a Montessori preschool, among many other community accomplishments. The government has rewarded their local initiatives by prioritizing the community for its own development plans as well.

Conclusion

ToP participatory strategic planning is a highly versatile process that builds on a natural human problem-solving journey to articulate a vision, face the underlying contradictions blocking that vision, design effective strategies, and implement strategic actions effectively. This method not only produces practical results, but it has the possibility of transforming the group who participates in the process.

As technology and forms of human interaction change, adaptation of the process will continue. When these adaptations are based on the underlying phenomenological method, they will continue to have profound results.

Practical resources

A very useful resource for details about the strategic thinking and planning process is the book *Transformational Strategy* by Bill Staples[58]. A training course is also available[59].

---

58 Staples, 2012

59 http://www.ica-associates.ca/product/transformational-strategy/ or see http://www.ica-international.org/ica-worldwide to find training in other countries

8.
Action Planning

Until one is committed, there is hesitancy, the chance to draw back, always ineffectiveness. Concerning all acts of initiative (and creation), there is one elementary truth, the ignorance of which kills countless ideas and splendid plans: that the moment one definitely commits oneself, then Providence moves too. All sorts of things occur to help one that would never otherwise have occurred. A whole stream of events issues from the decision, raising in one's favour all manner of unforeseen incidents and meetings and material assistance, which no man could have dreamt would have come his way. I have learned a deep respect for one of Goethe's couplets:

Whatever you can do, or dream you can, begin it.
Boldness has genius, power, and magic in it!

—William Hutchison Murray[60]

A very small organization had only two employees who were having difficulties working together and asked for a strategic plan. However, they had only half a day to make the plan. Upon asking detailed questions about their needs, it became clear that they really didn't need a strategic plan at all—they needed to separate their roles and to trust that the other person was doing the operational tasks the organization needed. After clarifying their roles, each one worked through the action planning workbook, clarifying the accomplishments they needed for their role in the next six months, and timelining the specific actions that would get them there. They shared the action plans on a common timeline and agreed to meet weekly to check their progress and provide support to one another. At the end of the morning, they had created a solid shared plan and their working relationship had already improved.

At the other end of the scale, after a major participatory strategic planning process that involved hundreds of people, the dean of a university department asked for volunteers to plan the implementation of the strategies. Each implementation planning team included a resource person and up to

---

60 Murray, 1951

20 volunteers. Each group worked through the action planning workbook on large posters on the wall, identifying strengths, weaknesses, dangers, and benefits of working on the strategy. This modified SWOT analysis focused the strategy toward inspiring and practical accomplishments for three years, two years, and one year with six-month milestones. Then they brainstormed, sequenced and timelined actions toward the six-month and one-year accomplishments. The last two steps named the people who would work on the action plans and the estimated costs. It was very clear that the actions had been seriously thought through. At the plenary session, after reports and clarifications of each action plan, the dean approved the resources needed for implementation. Within days the groups plunged into their actions.

Background

The *action planning method* was originally designed for task forces to work on projects of all kinds. Its origins came from a method called "Maneuvering," from the image of maneuvering around obstacles to get to the destination. It was used to involve people in making workable plans for village projects, for detailed planning for setting up global conferences and think tanks, and for carrying out weekly team projects.

In the 1980s, the action planning method was formally laid out in a workbook form to help client groups plan short-term projects and operational plans. In the 1990s, ICA Canada evolved a variation of the process with participatory strategic planning. When we did this, we began to call the simpler action planning process *task force action planning* to distinguish between the two forms.

This chapter focuses first on the simpler action planning process. If you want to do action planning as part of strategic planning, read Chapter 7 and then take a special look at the variation on page 96.

Brief description

The ToP action planning method takes people through a solid thinking process to choose a practical yet inspiring accomplishment for a period of time on a project that is ready to proceed. The *intentional focus* is on practical action toward a measurable result. The *method of inquiry* is a discovery process that participants work through to choose the accomplishment and the actions to get there in *radical openness* to what inspires the group.

The basic process has nine steps:
1. Identify what victory would look like if the project were accomplished.
2. Examine the current reality that supports or limits activity on the project internally and externally, in the present and the future (a modified SWOT analysis using strengths and weaknesses, benefits and dangers).
3. In light of the current reality, state the bottom-line accomplishment that the group is committed to.
4. Brainstorm a list of appropriate concrete actions needed to accomplish that result.
5. Organize the actions by sequencing them and perhaps clustering similar actions together.

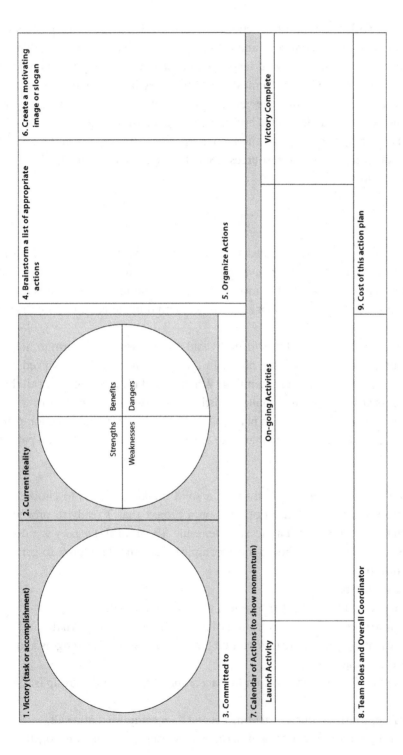

FIGURE 11

Overview of the action planning workbook

6. Create an image or slogan that will motivate the team.
7. Put the actions on a timeline, identifying a launch activity and ongoing activities, with the accomplishment as the result at the end of the timeline.
8. Name the team and their roles, including the overall coordinator or champion.
9. Project the costs (time and money) of the plan.

Through the process, the group takes responsibility for making the actions happen. The carefully designed sequence of steps systematically builds group capacity to accomplish the tasks:

- Clarify and delineate the tasks
- Align the creativity, capabilities, interests, and resources of the group
- Determine the necessary actions, roles, and responsibilities
- Build group trust, support, enthusiasm, and consensus
- Create an implementation timeline to accomplish the task
- Coordinate actions and assignments
- Build group trust, support, enthusiasm, and consensus
- Create an implementation timeline to accomplish the task
- Coordinate actions and assignments.

The process is generally done on a series of worksheets. This easily customizable approach allows flexibility in the steps of the process so that any information that becomes clear at the later stages can be incorporated into the final outcome.

Figure 11 shows a summary or overview that combines the three worksheets in the basic action planning workbook. There are three steps on each worksheet.

Purpose

The overall purpose of the action planning process is to simplify the creation of concrete realistic and inspiring plans that are strong enough to make change happen. The steps help a group avoid common traps and plan actions that will really be carried out and accomplish their aims.

Project planning

The action planning process works well as a participatory tool to define the focus of a project and choose the actions that will accomplish the aims. After capturing the big picture of the project's objectives in the Victory Circle, the work in the current reality exercise applies a reality check, helping participants choose the bottom line that the group is committed to accomplishing. Then the step-by-step identifying of the major actions, sequencing them, and putting them on the timeline allows the group to create its own actions. The slogan or symbol step creates sustained motivation and brings the team together in a non-verbal way.

Implementation stage of strategic planning

When a group has thought through vision and obstacles and created strategies, the next human question is how the strategies will be accomplished. A team is assigned to carry out each strategy and build a plan for it. A variation of the action planning process starts with the strategy and the details of the cards behind it, followed by a current reality exercise to ground the strategy in the real world. From there the group brainstorms several possible accomplishments and chooses one major measureable accomplishment for a designated time period, usually three to six months. Then they think through the actions and sequence them on a timeline. They also design a motivating slogan or symbol for the action campaign. The last important step is to identify the team, including a champion or lead, and to estimate costs in time and money. When all the teams have completed the process, all of the action plans are put on a wall timeline, and the whole group adjusts the complete plan for all the strategies and their interrelationships and affirms their commitment.

The phenomenology behind action planning

At its core, action planning is similar to strategic planning. It starts with articulating the big picture of a future direction that is already in participants' minds, then examines the current situation, including internal strengths and weaknesses and external benefits and dangers, and finally, it uses that information to create an accomplishment or commitment that is grounded in reality. Only then can a group create the detailed specific actions that will make that grounded commitment happen.

The action planning process envisions a preferred future, acknowledges reality and our associations with it, and then explores implications and makes choices that move from more abstract to more concrete at each step.

The *intentional focus* of the action planning process is to keep actions grounded in reality, while also inspiring participation. The *method of inquiry* moves from objectifying the big picture of the vision, through the complexities of the current reality to a realistic yet compelling commitment, and then articulating the practical actions that will make their vision a reality. The naming of the team and the cost provide another reality check before the process is finished, and the flexibility of the workbook allows the planning group to move back to earlier stages if they discover they have missed something. Doing this planning in small groups also keeps the planning more honest, both by staying focused on the intention of the strategy or project, and also in "right-sizing" the work so they don't take on too much or too little.

Design patterns

Action planning moves through three parts, as shown in the overview Figure 11 on page 90.

Part One: Victory, current reality, and commitment

The first three steps help people articulate the tension between future hopes and the present reality in order to create grounded commitment to specific outcomes.

Victory circle

Ask the group to imagine that they are standing at the end of the process in a victory circle, like at the end of a horse race, when the champagne is pouring, and to articulate what they see. This exercise creates a visual short-term vision of the results and their impact, and projects the desired results beyond boring tasks.

Current reality

The current reality grid asks the group to do a quick modified SWOT analysis, reflecting on their strengths and weaknesses in relation to the victory, and the benefits and dangers of moving toward that victory. This step acknowledges the reality of the current situation, and transforms resistance into important information for ensuring success.

There has been much discussion around the four sections of the SWOT analysis. The major intention is to clarify the current situation, both internal and external, as it relates to the victory, as well as the potential future. Strengths and weaknesses focus on the current situation. You can use either benefits and dangers, or opportunities and threats, to clarify your thinking about the future.

Commitment

The commitment step builds on the vision and current reality to focus the group on what they are willing to commit to accomplishing. Stating the commitment ensures that the group's plans are grounded in reality, both realistic and inspiring, and creates a foundation for success.

Part Two: Brainstorming and organizing actions and motivation

The middle three steps begin the process of imagining how the commitment will be accomplished.

Brainstorming and sequencing steps

Brainstorming a list of appropriate actions provides the creative input for what to do. The separate analytical process of combining and sequencing the steps provides the opportunity to make sure they will work and sets up the timelining step in the next part. This process provides a rich list of practical actions.

Motivating image or slogan

Creating a motivating image or slogan allows the group to step back from the detailed, rational thinking process of organizing actions, and to use visual and metaphorical intelligence to enrich the creation of a campaign that group members can stand behind.

Part Three: Timing, roles and cost

The last three steps ground the commitment and actions in reality, which increases the likelihood that the actions will be done.

Calendar

Populating the calendar with actions from the brainstormed list shows the sequence of actions visually, including the launch activity, ongoing activities, and what the victory they have committed to will look like when complete. Often new or adapted actions emerge at this stage, as the impact of each action on the next becomes visible.

Roles

Writing the names of real people in their team roles and naming the overall coordinator is critical.

Whole Group	Rational Aim(s)	Experiential Aim(s)		
	clear, step-by-step action plans for each strategic direction; a coordinated overall action plan	commitment to a defined task; motivation to accomplish tasks		

Whole Group	Action Planning Participant's Workbook			Whole Group	
	Brainstorm	Cluster	Name		
Introduction	**Determine the measurable accomplishment**	**Decide on the SPECIFIC actions**	**Create the action timeline**	**Coordinate the group's plans**	**Conclusion**
Copy Action Planning manual for each participant. 1. Open the workshop 2. Give the context 3. Determine the time span of the planning period 4. Make assignments to action planning teams 5. Introduce the action planning manual: • Write "finishing date" on line 7 • Divide timeline in step 16 into time blocks and label with dates 6. Tell people how much time they have to work.	1. Write the name of the Strategy on the line. 2. List strengths 3. List weaknesses 4. List benefits 5. List dangers 6. Brainstorm possible accomplishments… 7. Write down Measurable Accomplishment by (date)	8. Write down Strategy 9. Copy Measurable Accomplishment (from step 7). 10. List the specific actions… 11. If more than ten actions are listed in step 10, organize into clusters… 12. Number cluster actions… 13. Create a motivating image or slogan…	14. Write down Strategy 15. Copy Meas. Acc. 16. Write actions in timeline 17. Name Implementation Team 18. Write down costs Copy Meas. Acc. (15), actions (16), Implem. Team (17), costs (18), each on a separate card. Put on wall timeline for plenary session. Add slogan or symbol if the team has one.	**Introduce plenary process** **One team reports (uninterrupted)** 1. Meas. Accomp. 2. Actions summary 3. Cost 4. Implem. team 5. Slogan/symbol **Whole group responds** 1. Questions of clarity 2. *Is this the accomplishment we need? (adjust)* 3. *Are these the actions that will make it happen? (adjust)* 4. Celebrate! Repeat for each team. **Final Consensus** 1. *Is this the overall plan we need? (adjust)* 2. Celebrate!	Reflect on the workshop **Next steps** • Documenting • Evaluating progress **Announcements** Closing
40 min.	30 min.	20 min.	30 min.	90 min.	30 min.

FIGURE 12

The procedures for the Canadian action planning process

As people see that they have declared their commitment publicly, it becomes even more clear who is really committed to this action plan, and therefore its viability and likelihood of success. If there is a team with a coordinator or champion, the responsibility is shared, and people feel less overwhelmed.

Cost in money and time

The final reality check is to estimate the cost and time of this action plan, and if necessary, where the resources are coming from. Sometimes this clarifies the need to alter the action plan by restricting the actions or the accomplishment, or adding new actions to round up the resources.

Design pattern variations

The main value to hold in advancing the use of a method like this is to keep the underlying shape or form: the big picture of the future, an analysis of current reality, commitment generation, and detailed steps. Separating these major kinds of brain activity unravels the complexity of thought, easing the process and helping avoid common traps in planning.

Online teamwork

The workbooks are flexible, and can be used online in platforms where forms can be completed by a group or a scribe for a group. For example, they can be used in a Microsoft PowerPoint upload to the whiteboard in Blackboard Collaborate or another synchronous online platform for a team to work on virtually.

Planning a project

A task force of the ToP Facilitator Network charged with creating virtual facilitation products met online and created a project charter that identified several areas of activity. Then small teams assigned to each work activity used the workbook to create a practical plan for achieving results in their area of activity.

Implementing a strategic plan

At the last stage of a strategic planning process, the Regent Park Community Health Centre needed to build an action plan for each of their strategies. The Executive Director and her leadership team decided to assign strategies to the working teams they had created within the organization, to strengthen and support the new team model. The Board of Directors was assigned to build an action plan to find a new building, and staff teams were assigned to other strategies. Within several years, the Board had addressed all the difficult challenges of getting the funding and permissions to build a new building, and construction had started.

Clarifying tasks within an organization

A small organization had three staff members with overlapping job descriptions. They were getting in each other's way while they worked and were losing momentum. First they clarified each person's responsibilities. Working individually, they each used the action planning workbook to plan the next three months of work. They each drew images of the results (victory) they hoped to attain through their own work. Next they examined their strengths and weaknesses to make that vision happen, and the external benefits and dangers involved in accomplishing the vision. This exercise helped them narrow down what they were truly committed to. When they shared these commitments with each other, they were able to make sure they were aligned but not overlapping. Working on their own again, they each brainstormed the actions needed to accomplish that vision, sequenced them, and let that part simmer a bit while they created a motivating slogan for their own action campaign. Then on the third page of the workbook they each chose a launch action and described what the results would look like in three months. Finally, they each wrote their names beside the actions they would do, and assessed the resources it would take to do it. In less than a half day, they had not only sorted out their separate responsibilities, but each of them had a carefully planned direction to kick-start a new sense of accomplishment.

The Canadian action planning process

A major variation on the design pattern of action planning evolved in the work of ICA Associates Inc. in Toronto. We took the basic workbook and began to use it as the implementation process for ToP strategic planning. This process is shown in the overview diagram in Figure 12, and the template for the complete workbook is in the Appendix on pages 181-184. Groups struggled with different parts, and we added specific steps to ease the transition between stages. We also replaced the "victory circle" with the name of the strategy. The strategy and the cards behind it can play the role of "victory" because embedded in them are the hopes and dreams of what is possible. The group needs to understand that they don't have to do every single action in the strategy, but they can see them together as the dynamic vision, which will evolve as they implement the strategy.

Review and re-planning after implementation

A part of the action planning process that occurs after the implementation is underway is the review and re-planning stage. At the end of the time period that the group has chosen, it is very helpful for the group to gather again to reflect on what happened during the implementation period. A journey wall of the elapsed time since the planning of the actions (see page 119) is very helpful here, as it includes everything that happened during the time period as well as what the actions the group carried out from its plans. They can celebrate their accomplishments and note the obstacles that held them back, extracting what they have learned from the experience. Some groups will find that their plans were too ambitious, and will be able to be more realistic the next time they plan. Other groups will realize that their plans were not ambitious enough, and will see that they can plan bigger for the next period of time. At this point, the group can use the workbook to plan for the next period of time and coordinate their new plans.

Another way to do the review is found in the strategic planning chapter on page 80.

Comparison with other approaches to operational planning

As background for a course on understanding planning systems, we recently did extensive internet research on operational planning. This search revealed very little clear methodology for making concrete plans that will actually work and provide a basis for accountability. Project planning tools create timelines of action, but there is little process for analysis to choose which accomplishments and actions will make the biggest difference.

Many people write goals and objectives for their work. Again, there is little process for analyzing possible goals, and often the stated goals and objectives are abstract or vague. The action planning process is one of the clearest ways to do operational planning because it clarifies the core steps of planning and articulates a measureable deliverable. In this case, the context starts out with a mandate or area of responsibility, and the workbook process is focused on that mandate.

Achieving authentic consensus

You need to prepare thoroughly in advance to ensure that the group can create grounded, well-thought-through action plans.

1. Preparing the workbook

You can find templates for both approaches to action planning in the appendix on pages 177-184.

You can customize the workbook if needed for your situation. If a client needs to think long-term as well as short-term, you can add an extra page for listing longer-term accomplishments as well as short-term ones. Some groups like to have a three-year action plan, as well as a two-year and a one-year plan, with six-month milestones.

2. Decide your milestones

It is best to set the first accomplishment or measurable milestone not more than six months in the future. Three to six months is a long enough period to accomplish something and see momentum, while not being so long that people get tired or bored of moving in the same direction. Lived history evolves so fast that it is helpful to review the situation in six months, celebrate accomplishments to sustain the momentum, and re-plan for the next 6 months.

Figure 13 shows how the wall looks with the final results at the end of the plenary of an action planning process.

Ensuring participation

1. Setting the atmosphere

The room setup needs to allow breakout groups to work simultaneously on different action plans. A wall timeline for the final stage needs to be able to be seen by all the participants. One helpful way of arranging the room is to have a round table for each action planning team to work around, and place them so that each person can see the working wall timeline.

If you are using the process for project planning, remind the group of their prior decision to do the project. Then review and list any basic decisions they've already made on a flip chart—who, what,

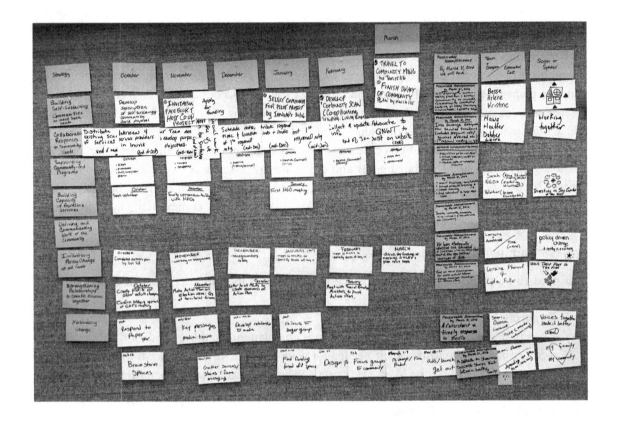

FIGURE 13

Each row is an action plan for a separate strategy or project, named on the left. The white cards are actions. The measurable accomplishment for each action plan is on a purple card in the third column from the right. Next to it is the named team and the cost estimate. The final row on the right is the slogan or symbol for each action campaign.

when, and so on. Discuss the parameters of the project so that everyone understands exactly what the project is, the anticipated time frame, and who the stakeholders or participants will be. Remind the group of the importance of the project, its purpose, the linkage to other work of the organization, and any other pertinent context. Convey excitement about doing the project with your voice and energy.

2. Give the instructions

Walk through the whole workbook with an example, having people put their own data on the appropriate steps as you go, such as strategy or project name and dates. This helps people understand the process, and be more ready to participate.

3. Ways to engage people

The people who are planning the actions need to be the people who will carry them out, as much as possible, to ensure that their commitment to do the actions is real. When deciding who works on which action plan, factor in volunteer passion by having people choose which action plan they would like to work on. In some situations it helps to assign people to work on the one that relates most closely to their role or job description. Some combination of these approaches is optimal.

Achieving high quality results

Successful action planning takes time. The simplest action planning workbook can often be done in less than an hour, but the more complex versions take at least a half hour for the first page, and 45 minutes for the last two pages if done thoroughly. And the more thorough the planning is, the more likely that the plans will work and be carried out.

It is wise, generally, to have not more than one measureable accomplishment per short-term plan. Most people cannot accomplish more than one new thing in three to six months. You can quote us on this: "History does not change from the big things we *ought* to do. History changes from the little things we *actually* do."

Many people need to have a longer-term accomplishment to aim for as well as short-term milestones along the way. Longer term may mean up to three years—beyond that the group is really creating a vision and the strategic planning process may be more useful.

The minimum effective action planning team is two or three people, for both creativity in generating the plan and support in doing the actions. Having more than five or six working on a plan makes the planning slower, but when they begin the actions, it can also spread the workload of the actions to make it more doable.

Often the working teams go through the whole workbook process in one session, which takes about an hour and a half. Another approach that can help the groups stay in sync as they work is to stop after all teams have completed the first page, have them share the accomplishments they have identified, and check for consistency. Then teams reconvene to finish the process and share their plan on a common timeline.

When several action planning teams are working simultaneously, often each plan affects those of other teams. Sometimes it is helpful to stop and share the commitments of each team before they go on to create the actions, to make sure that each team is on track and that there is no overlap among them. A plenary session coordinating all the plans can be very effective in preventing duplication and creating mutual support. Figure 13 on page 98 is from a final plenary session.

Sometimes a group selects a project that everyone needs to have input into, and they sometimes ask to do the planning process together as a large group. This is possible, and the conversation will be very deep, but they need to know that the consequence is that they will need more time to finish the process.

Addressing the existential aim

The teams who will carry out the actions need to be the same people who plan the actions wherever possible: this approach creates more grounded and realistic commitment as well as excitement about working together. People are not as likely to do actions that someone else plans for them as they are to do the ones that they themselves plan to do.

The step that asks for weaknesses and either threats or dangers acknowledges the obstacles in moving forward, which provides an outlet for expressing reluctance and the wisdom that creates it. The step that asks for strengths and benefits balances the obstacles with reasons for moving forward. Answering this combination of questions can unblock people's resistance while using their wisdom to keep the final outcome realistic.

The symbol or slogan step often seems silly at first glance, but it turns a boring timeline into an action campaign and can serve as an ongoing motivator. Teams who don't do this step in their working groups often create one when they see other teams' symbols or slogans being posted on the plenary wall. Jokes and laughter often result. Usually they create a sense of teamwork with the implementation team. One group, tasked with recruiting hospital volunteers, used their slogan, "Have a (heart), Volunteer" as a banner hung on the exterior hospital wall facing a major highway as a recruitment tactic, so the slogan took on a larger role than just to motivate the team.

The step that asks for the names of the people committed to carrying out the actions makes the plan very real—it is at this point where people suddenly say, "Oh, you really meant that we will carry out this plan!" If no one wants to do the action plan, you can go back to the second step and note that "no one wants to do this," and then adjust either the accomplishment or the actions so that the group is committed to doing them. The intention is not to create unrealistic expectations or guilt, but to create realistic (and inspiring) plans that will succeed and make a difference. The self-story that "I can't do anything about my situation" is replaced with "Yes we can!"

Impacts of this method

Often, groups discover that they have accomplished considerably more than they thought they could when they review their progress at the end of the time period they planned for. As Scottish mountaineer and writer William Hutchison Murray said, "the moment one definitely commits oneself, then Providence moves too" (full quote on page 88). When the group isn't able to accomplish what they intended, a reflective review at the end of the time period acknowledges the unexpected obstacles and uses the experience to learn about what makes effective planning and action in their situation.

Sometimes groups create aspirational plans that are much larger than they can reasonably accomplish. An affirmative review process helps the group learn how to do more realistic plans.

When task teams implement specific plans and the results are vetted in a plenary, the group builds trust that its parts can work on their own. This success reduces the tendency for others to try to micromanage the work of the teams.

Short-term planning, such as for a three- to six-month time period, adds urgency to vague long-term objectives, and breaks the big goals into bite-size accomplishments. Celebration of short-term accomplishments and mid-course corrections adds momentum and sustains commitment to a longer-term project.

Examples of action planning

Large scale action planning

When I was working with the large education department at the University of Toronto's Ontario Institute for Studies in Education (OISE), many people wanted to get involved in the action planning. A team of 20 was created for each action plan, and participants signed up, along with a designated resource person and a champion. A large copy of the workbook template for the first page was posted on the wall. Together the team of 20 worked through the template to identify several accomplishments they wanted to see. Then smaller groups within each action planning team worked on detailed actions for each accomplishment. With representatives from all the teams, they shared the accomplishments from all the groups in a separate plenary. The work was so well thought through that the dean approved all the action plans on the spot.

Personal unblocking through action planning

An individual asked for help with some life planning. She had a vague idea of where she wanted to get to, but was blocked in moving on it. Working through the simple workbook, starting with drawing images of her vision of herself already living the future she envisioned, gave her a practical plan to get started on, and the thought of doing periodic review to revise her plans removed the block of thinking she had to have all the right answers at the beginning.

Individual action planning was also used in a training course for employment. People created personal action plans for getting a job as a part of their training. The employment trainer noted that participants were much more successful in getting started on finding a job.

Project planning

Planners often struggle with how to create stakeholder "buy-in" to the project plans. If the stakeholders co-create the plans, they feel they "own" them, and nothing has to be "bought" or "sold". The first page of the action planning workbook helps with the first steps of collaboratively creating a project charter, and the rest of the workbook is valuable for creating the actions.

Accountability framework

One health organization asked for a process to involve a wide variety of stakeholders in creating an accountability framework that was mandated by the territorial government. They were used to planning goals, which were generally abstract and unattainable. They used the action planning process as a template, but much of the language was adapted to use their wording and extra steps were added to achieve the results they wanted. After an initial exercise at the beginning agreed on strategic priorities, the group moved on to identify measurable outcomes (for which accountability could be held) for each strategic priority. A page was added to connect each measurable outcome with indicators of success and the impact it would have on the community. Then they identified specific actions and put them on a timeline. The result was a set of clear measurable outcomes and actions toward them that were not only sufficient to meet the mandate from government but helped them achieve health outcomes in their region.

Implementation planning for mandated tasks

A regional department of the federal government asked for implementation planning for their team's mandates from the ministry. Their customized workbook started with exploring their mandate, and then moved on to creating deliverables for each mandate, followed by actions needed to accomplish the deliverables. Since they also had to implement their strategic plan, a page was added that connected the deliverables to their strategy and vision. In this way, they could see how working on their operational plans for their mandated work could be done in such a way as to also carry out their strategies and move toward their vision. They were much more hopeful that they could accomplish what was expected of them while making a difference in the region with their actions.

Conclusion

In summary, if you are looking for a practical participatory planning process that combines big picture thinking with detailed, logical planning, the action planning method can make the process smooth and effective. And if you want to ensure that your strategic directions can be implemented, it can help with that, too.

Practical resources

Use the templates starting on page 177.

The basic action planning method is taught in the US in their Group Facilitation Methods course[61] and in Canada as Task Force Action Planning in the Advanced ToP Tools course.[62] The variation used in Canada in the implementation stage of strategic planning is taught in the Transformational Strategy course.[63]

---

61 https://icausa.memberclicks.net/top-facilitation-methods
62 http://www.ica-associates.ca/product/advanced-top-tools/
63 http://www.ica-associates.ca/product/transformational-strategy/

9.
The ToP Journey Wall

Not I, not I, but the wind that blows through me!
A fine wind is blowing the new direction of Time.
If only I let it bear me, carry me, if only it carry me!
If only I am sensitive, subtle, oh, delicate, a winged gift!
If only, most lovely of all, I yield myself and am borrowed
By the fine, fine wind that takes its course through the chaos of the world
Like a fine, an exquisite chisel, a wedge-blade inserted;
If only I am keen and hard like the sheer tip of a wedge
Driven by invisible blows,
The rock will split, we shall come at the wonder, we shall find the Hesperides.

—D.H. Lawrence[64]

The rock will split: Wayne's story

In 1978, I joined the staff of ICA's community development project in Nigeria. As I arrived and settled in, it became apparent that the previous year had been a rough one for the staff. Difficulties beyond their control seemed to interrupt their work constantly. People told me stories about crises and troubles of nearly every nature possible to such an organization. A couple of key staff members had left the project and morale was pretty low. It was apparent that many positive things were happening in the community, but they seemed lost in the fog of the team's negative story.

When the time to do project action planning for the next year rolled around on the calendar, I found myself assigned to guide our planning retreat. It was clear to me that the team needed to look back, see their situation more clearly, and make some sense of the chaotic experience of the past year. They certainly needed to identify and acknowledge their challenges and difficulties so they

---

64 Lawrence, 1959. From the poem "Song of a Man Who Has Come Through"

could move beyond them. They needed to rediscover the real success and progress they had made. They needed a new way to see their situation and tell their story that would release them to engage and be more effective in the following year.

I chose to begin the planning process with a journey wall. The method had been developed quite recently and I was keen to try this new application. I began by drawing a horizontal line on our blackboard and divided it into 12 segments, one for each month of the past year. I then divided the group into six working groups of two or three people and asked each group to brainstorm five to ten events that were significant for the group. After working in small groups, we wrote each event on the timeline under the appropriate date.

What a full year it was! We filled the board with over 50 events the group felt were significant. The number itself was a bit of a surprise to everyone, because they felt not much had really happened.

As we looked at the events, we identified which ones were accomplishments and noted those that were clearly setbacks. As we talked about the year, many stories were told. Events that had slipped from memory were remembered. The atmosphere in the room began to shift from hesitation to fascination as people became more engaged.

I asked the group to describe their mood over the course of the year. It seemed to have begun on a positive note with a lot of possibilities. I placed the chalk on the board about two-thirds of the way up and asked the group to help me complete the line throughout the whole year. The "mood line" started fairly high and quickly dropped over the next couple of months following a negative experience with a government agency. The line slowly rose as the focus was placed on a couple of quite successful projects. It dropped again during an especially ambiguous chaotic time and began to rise quite rapidly as the community street lighting project illuminated the night. We sifted through the timeline and marked several events as significant. The group found that the majority of the events they named as significant were more positive than negative.

We looked again at the events on the timeline, this time considering the ones that seemed to indicate shifts in our work, our results and the overall mood. We found three major shifts. After looking at each of the four time periods, we gave a title to each to describe the experience. This being a rough year, I was prepared to hear titles filled with doom and despair. The group had become so entangled in the frustrating challenges that it was difficult to see their whole situation and its significance.

But I was surprised. They titled the first period "Looking Down the Road to Victory." The second was "The Rock in the Middle of the Road." The third period was "Crushed but Climbing." And they called the final time period, the last six weeks, "Beginning to Move." These titles reflected the events identified as well as the flow of mood and spirit in the group.

As we looked at the whole timeline, I asked the group to give the whole year a title. It was clear that the question was now looking beyond the timeline itself. They were looking at their actual lived experience of the past year.

It was not an easy conversation, but people were able to see that they had actually made significant progress in their work with the community itself. The realization came somewhat slowly until we began to give it a name. Someone called out, "The Rock Will Split" a line from the D.H. Lawrence poem that begins this chapter—a poem about moving into, through and beyond a personal existential crisis. When the group heard those words, their whole image of the past year shifted from one of defeat to perseverance in the face of real, difficult, traumatic and challenging times. The mood in the group went through the ceiling.

The rock did indeed split. Not only did it become the title for a time period, but it became a kind of rallying cry. They knew, deep inside themselves, that they would not accept defeat, but they needed to look deeply into their situation and their attitudes toward it to discover their deeper, more powerful story of what was happening. This exercise truly transformed the whole group's relationship to their work and their future.

Brief description

The journey wall exercise is also known as the "wall of wonder" and "historical scan." We believe the name "journey wall" best holds the intention of the method that helps people examine their journey from different perspectives and in a larger context. The group creates together a shared story of the meaning of their journey to this point. From here, they see the next steps of their journey as influenced by but not solely determined by what's happened so far.

The journey wall exercise has five major steps that are laid out in Figure 14:

1. Introducing the exercise
2. Recalling significant events
3. Reflecting on lived experience

Steps in the ToP Journey Wall				
Introducing the exercise	**Recalling significant events**	**Reflecting on lived experience**	**Telling the common story**	**Concluding The workshop**
Welcome and introductions Setting the strategic context Introducing the journey wall	Individual brainstorm Group brainstorm Create the timeline	Reflective conversation Identify key turning points Determine major phases	Name each section Name the whole timeline	Reflect on the workshop Build a bridge to the future Closing

FIGURE 14

The steps of the ToP journey wall method

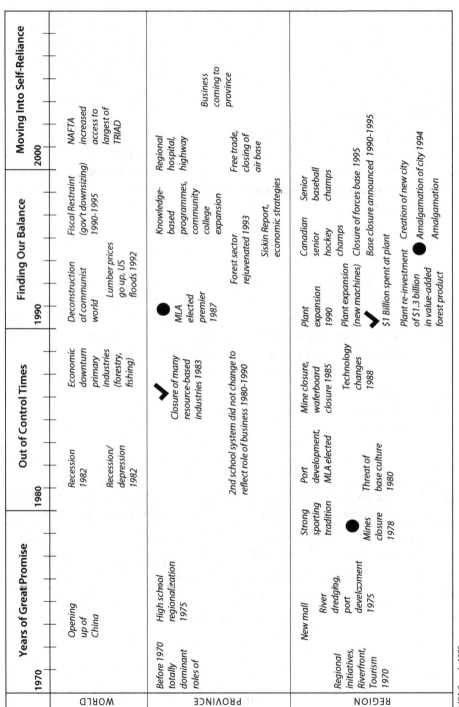

FIGURE 15

Sample journey wall created in a workshop with a community looking back on the previous decades

4. Telling the common story

5. Concluding the exercise

The steps and the design patterns behind them are described in more detail below. It can be quite powerful for an organization or community to rethink their history in a journey wall exercise.

Figure 15 shows a sample product from a journey wall done with a community some years ago. This community discovered through the process that their struggles had brought significant change and they became hopeful about the future.

Background

When we are about to try something new, we search through our experience for clues that might help us decide how to proceed. We stand in the "now" and look from our past, our "now-no-longer" into the future, our "now-not-yet." The ToP journey wall exercise prepares a group to weave the threads of its history into the fabric of its future. Participants recall and recreate experience that has been forgotten or become difficult to discuss openly. The exercise provides an opportunity for the group to clearly see how their actions and the events in their common life have shaped their current situation. Because it opens the group to the awe of its own experience, some facilitators have called the ToP journey wall the "wall of wonder." Others have focused on the analytic nature and called it the "historical scan."

The journey wall process is often used as an early step in a strategy planning process in order to provide a platform for helping the group envision its future.

It can also focus on monitoring and assessing strategic action, helping a group look at its events, achievements, tangible results, substantial impact and the significance of short-term actions. Again, it can focus on emerging trends, strategic position and scenarios for emergent strategy. The scan process can also be an inquiry into learning lessons from experience, identifying best practices, and designing innovative approaches. Each of these purposes can be accomplished in forms ranging from a few reflective questions to a substantial conversation or a full journey wall exercise.

The phenomenology behind the journey wall method

The journey wall steps follow the same underlying pattern as the focused conversation and workshop methods. The events are the objective level, the high and low points are the reflective level, discerning turning points in the journey is the interpretive level, and naming the phases and the whole are the decisional level.

Sharing lived experience

The *intentional focus* of the journey wall is on events in the lived experience of the participants. These events are things that have actually happened and are related to the group and its inquiry. By recalling significant events, the group grounds the inquiry in reality and enables participants to relate to what has happened in their common life and work. They bring their past into this moment and experience it together. The initial reflection enables the group to discern patterns in their experience ranging from determinative events, moods, transition points and major phases. Further reflection helps the group create a meaningful narrative of their existence together and places them in position to face their future. They stand in and acknowledge the reality of their situation.

The exercise then steps beyond or transcends the objective facts and events to examine the mood, the quality of their experience, their basic assumptions and the relationship the group has taken to their situation. Discussion and exploration of shared experience reduces social distance and opens the group to collaborative conversation. Talking about the events together provides a reflective platform that opens the potential for organizational learning. It allows the group to enliven its history by articulating its significance and enables them to create a story that imbues their experience and purpose with meaning. It also reveals options and choices to to which the group must relate. Participants grasp their future as open, and themselves as both free to explore its possibility and responsible for crafting their own future.

Creating a common story

The activity of doing a journey wall exercise enlivens history. People can, in a very short time, take their history off the dusty archive shelves and use it to help move into the future. Each person's story about past events changes, as other people name forgotten or ignored events, and interpretations of the meaning of the past are shared.

The journey wall process uses the knowledge and experience of the group to distill the significance of their history and create a meaningful story. It brings memory into living form by acknowledging significant events and telling the stories that have shaped the organization and its work. It enables the group to create its own legends and stories and create a mythology that aligns purpose, experience and action. A look at experience can heal wounds, resolve disputes and close gaps that keep people apart, freeing them to move forward together.

The journey wall enables people to build their own sense of continuity as they weave the future from the past. People are more likely to engage in creative thinking about the future when they see how their history is evolving and gain a sense of its importance. Reviewing experience in this way helps them envision how they want things to be.

These ways of talking about the organization, its purpose and its real history can provide a strong reference point for shaping an organization's culture, because they contain kernels of shared values and foundational understandings.

Learning from living

To be human is to be oriented toward the future; toward possibility—to be purposeful. This is *radical openness*. To move forward creatively and effectively, we need the perspectives and insight gained from experience. We stand in the present moment and look at the experience that has brought us to this point and describe our current situation in the world. The journey wall exercise enables groups to discern the substance and significance of past experience so they can learn from it and position themselves for the future. Standing before the reality of our situation informs our attitudes, relationships and choices.

The journey wall *method of inquiry* helps people focus on and appreciate their experience as they consider the future. When they see how their actions and the events in their lives have shaped their situation, real organizational learning can take place. Accomplishments and setbacks reveal critical lessons that can be applied to future plans. Acknowledging the effort it took to get the organization to this point brings closure to the past and opens possibility. The journey wall helps people build their own sense of continuity as they weave the future from the past. Starting from an understanding of what has actually taken place and how history is evolving helps people engage in grounded but creative thinking about the future.

Forming common bonds

Shared experience is a powerful bonding agent. A collection of individuals focused on a common purpose can become a group with its own being and the capacity to grasp its experience and step beyond it. An appreciative look at the past strengthens those natural connections. A look at experience can heal wounds, resolve disputes and close gaps that keep people apart, freeing them to move forward together. Pride in accomplishment, reflection on difficulties, insights into effectiveness and a common story all bring people together in a closer relationship with their common purpose. In coming together as an entity with being, a group can transcend its experience, imagine alternatives, make plans and choices and create itself in totally new ways.

Design patterns

Each of the five major steps in the journey wall exercise is composed of specific design patterns, preceded by specific tailoring and preparation. These design patterns are used in other ToP applications, too; here they're adapted to the specific purpose of journey walls.

The journey wall process is methodologically rich, complex and flexible. It integrates a great deal of objective and personal information as well as revealing insight into the operations, organization and culture of the group. It enables a group to make sense of its experience and take a clear, conscious relationship to it. It provides a foundation from which the group can move into the future. In this section we will explore the journey wall exercise through the lens of the four levels of ToP phenomenology.

Preparation: The key to success

Tailoring the journey wall exercise

Ask enough questions to gain a thorough understanding of the contextual framework while you work with the client to tailor the process to their needs. As a neutral presence, you will be able to describe the full situation within which the group is working.

Clarifying the aims of the scan and the allotted scope of the timeline helps you focus the attention of the participants. The *rational aim* tells you what kinds of insights you will ask for in the reflective discussion after the timeline is complete, such as trends that emerge from the data, or lessons learned. The *experiential aim* names how the participants need to be different as a result of the exercise. For example, they might need to be able to appreciate the struggle they have been through, or have hope for the future (as in Wayne's story), or discover, as one Indigenous group did in a journey wall exercise, that they are a strong people that they can be proud of being.

The focal point of this scan is, of course, the historical timeline. You need two and a half to three metres (eight to ten feet) of flat, blank wall space for the timeline. Set up the room so that everyone can see the timeline on the wall clearly and are able to read the cards or sticky notes.

You need to think through the length of the time period to work with. The time period is key to releasing the group's energy for the future. It might be 500 years of Indigenous Health, 150 years of Inuit Education, or your parents' whole lives that puts their currently troubled relationship into perspective. For a contextual scan before a planning workshop, consider how long the organization has existed. Add a section for "before we began," and a section for the future. For a project review, start with the time period when the project was first conceived, unless previous events helped create the milieu. Divide the timeline into an appropriate number of time blocks—usually weeks, years or decades—and put the dates in each block.

For a journey wall focused on setting a broad context, you might want to include three or four rows of different levels of events—for example, a row for global events, one for the local community or organization, and between those rows one at a medium level, such as the region or the field. The events in the larger context will inform things that happened in the local community or organization, breaking the isolation or silos and opening the group to see the impact other factors have on them. For example, a global recession could illuminate the financial struggles of the organization that resulted in widespread layoffs.

Introducing the exercise

After a welcome and introduction, set a context to place the scan in the framework of the group's purpose, history, experience, needs and plans. The context establishes the importance of reflecting on and learning from the past. It adds significance to what is about to be done. It states the purpose of the exercise and indicates the role the results will play in the future. Then you can introduce the graphic timeline and establish the time frame so the participants are prepared to engage in the exercise. An easy way to begin using the timeline is to ask questions to identify a few key marking points to help people remember things that have happened. Before you go on, state and clarify the focus question for the exercise. The question for a journey wall is usually a specific variation of "What have been the significant events between a certain date and the present?"

Objective Level: Lived experience

Recalling significant events

This is where you focus on *events*. An understanding of any group's history begins with the events people see as important. The actual events that make up every human experience provide the basic information for an examination of what has brought the group to its present situation. This step grounds the group in the reality of their own experience by focusing directly on what has actually happened. It is different from feelings about the events or analysis of the events. At the objective level, the events are the concrete, tangible happenings that will provide a springboard for reflection. Doing this as a group expands the memory and is the beginning of making new meaning. Sometimes having documents or people who were around at the beginning of the timeline fills in gaps and avoids assumptions about the past.

An *event* is something tangible that happened and can be located in time and space. It would be possible to take a picture of it. It can be located on a calendar. A simple "who–what–when" story could be written about it. The most important element, in this case, is the "what" —the event itself.

"Two directors retired in 1985" is an event that happened.

"Cast adrift" is a feeling about the event.

"Leadership continuity is crucial" is an idea derived from reflection on that event.

Those thoughts are important, but the first emphasis is to identify the things that actually happened. At this point, reflection and judgment are held in suspension, so the group can build a foundation grounded on lived experience.

An important aspect of events is their *connectedness and significance to the topic*. Not all events are significant to all scans. A topic focus question will focus the brainstorm of events on those that might hold significance within the aim of the particular journey wall. For example, in a large, complex organization, many things happen that are significant to a specific project, but may have little relevance to many other aspects of the organization. If the aim is to review the project, the question would be "What have we done in relation to this project?" If the aim of the overall session is to formulate strategies, the organization's past accomplishments would be significant. If the aim is to analyze social trends in order to understand the needs that the organization need to address, you would focus on the events that influence the field or affect society.

There are many types of events. An event can be something that was planned and staged, like a public event or a meeting or a phone conversation with a person important to the group's work. It can be an event that marks a distinct achievement or notable setback. It can be an event that indicated a stage has been completed or a new stage launched. It can be something that happened beyond the organization entirely that impacted the organization.

All events are relevant and included without judgment. There is as much to be gained from a painful experience as from a happy one. The "temporary plant shutdown" can be just as important as the "new product announcement." Acknowledging all events can be vital to learning from the journey wall. "The big strike" might seem like a negative event to put on a timeline, but it might well be a key learning point from several different perspectives.

Brainstorming events

The first step is the brainstorm. Ask the group to identify significant events that have brought them to their current situation. Each individual makes their own list of events they see as significant. In some cases, you might ask the group to think of events that are accomplishments and setbacks in order to ensure a full impression of the group's real history. Small working groups share their ideas and form a common list of events. They write each event on a card with a marker in bold letters and the time period in pencil for easy reference. When you gather the group together you systematically get the event cards on the timeline, so they are visible to the whole group.

Read each card out loud and ask where it goes on the timeline if that's not clear. The group can ask questions of clarification or adjust the date. The placement of cards is often accompanied by storytelling to place an event itself in context or to clarify it for those who have not heard it. Recalling events and telling the stories about them deepens the group's common memory and bonds of connection.

Include the events on the timeline without judgment. Through seeing and reflecting on many specific events throughout its history, the group is able to see the patterns that form the whole of its experience.

The result of this step is a brainstorm of significant events displayed on a timeline. The group now has the basic information they need in order to reflect on their situation. Figure 16 shows the brainstorm step in progress.

When all the events are posted on the timeline, the group can see its history and experience laid out before them. The timeline brings reality up close, personal and immediate to each member of the group. Once an individual contributes an idea, it becomes a part of the group's reality. The timeline, as it is created, becomes a representation of shared experience, and a common history becomes conscious. It brings the past into a timeless present in which people can stand aside from their immediate experience and view it from a more detached perspective. The graphic display of events reveals history as grounded information about their life and work together. It objectifies their actual experience, triggers reflection and connections, and opens them deeper reflection about their situation.

Reflective Level: Reflecting on lived experience

Considering the common journey
The next major step in the journey wall enables the group to reflect on their experience and tell their story. First, the group reflects on the experience and significance of the events. Then, the group takes a look at their journey and tells the story of their history.

Group members have brainstormed events they perceive as significant. In the reflective part of the process, they more fully remember the events and all the activity and nuances surrounding them and bring them into the present moment. The reflective level of this exercise enables participants to describe the qualities of their collective experience and identify the major phases of their work together.

As we remember events, we recall our own experience of the events along with the mood and feelings of others and the whole group. The facilitator's questions are designed to help people remember their experience and express it. "I was saddened when I heard that the manager announced

FIGURE 16

Objective level of the journey wall, with cards naming events posted on the timeline

his retirement. I felt somewhat adrift." Questions allow people to explore and express their real feelings about how events affected them and the organization. In remembering, people literally reconstitute their experience. In articulating it, they step away from the events themselves, relate themselves to their experience, and begin seeing how it has affected their current situation.

We make a wide variety of connections among the events in our lives. We recall similarities with other things that have happened. We seek connections that reveal genuinely meaningful relationships among aspects of the group's experience.

One's history is the story of change, and this is no less true for a group. The timeline enables the group to see shifts in style, mood and ways of working over time. They can note changes in structures and policies. They can describe the development and life cycle of a project. They discover distinct turning points when a significant change altered the group's situation. In some cases, people will see events building up to a major change. Sometimes a major event will trigger a significant shift in the group. These might have to do with the group's work, mission and its organizational culture. Being able to see significant transitions helps the group see the major phases and describe their significance. In sharing and reflecting on their experience, the group begins forming a coherent story of their journey. In telling their story, people stand back beyond the actual events to look at the whole. As they name the phases of their journey, they form and express their attitude or way of relating to their experience as a whole.

Articulating the group's reactions

While the group looks at the timeline, you pose a series of reflective-level questions to draw out their internal reactions to the events on the timeline. Begin with noticing specific events that stand out among the others because of their impact and significance. People will note surprising or especially funny or tragic events. They will discover things they had forgotten or didn't know about, and they hear others' stories of things that have shaped the organization. Figure 17 captures the marking of high and low points in the group's experience of the events on the timeline.

Often some storytelling is necessary to help everyone understand specific events. The value of telling a series of quick stories within a time period is gaining a tangible sense of how things were at that time. It makes experience more real than unexpressed memory and provides substance, depth and texture, helping the participants make personal connections with their history. Sharing the stories brings them into the common memory and enables everyone to own them as the group's experience.

They remember issues and crises as well as victories and breakthroughs. They find that some time periods seem to have been eventful and fast-paced while others seem to have gone more slowly. They recall the mood of the group and the topics and tone of conversations in different times. To access metaphoric thinking, ask questions like, "What colour does this remind you of?" or "What weather system does it feel like?" or "What great epic drama could we be telling here?"

Consider asking the group to describe the general mood and tone throughout the period by drawing a line that moves up and down across the timeline as the group's mood changed, like a line graph. It can provide a graphic impression of how the group related to their situation as they moved through their history.

Ask people to identify events that were of special significance in order to bring focus to those happenings that shaped and defined the organization and the group. In many cases, it is helpful to ask the group to identify and mark key accomplishments and key setbacks to highlight the full spectrum of experience.

Interpretive Level: Telling the common story

Seeing the flow

Because individual events are shown in time sequence, the group will be able to see connections and associations among events that would not be possible without the graphic display. They may see changes in mood, style and organizational culture take place over time. The group might see

FIGURE 17

The reflective level of the journey wall exercise.

Note the up and down arrows showing people's experience of high and low points.

a sequence of events leading toward a change. They may see certain activities leading to disappointment and failure as well as the ways success was achieved. They see what happened, how it happened, how it affected them personally, and the role it played in their work and development as a group. The group looks beyond and through the events to discern patterns of meaning and significance. They see the state of their shared existence as it has unfolded.

Here you can ask the group to look for pivotal events that affected the group's identity or work. Pivotal events are those that catalyzed a transition, completed a phase, or launched a new one. The group reflects on the pace of change throughout its history to determine the characteristics of each part of the timeline. Among the high points and low points along the way, the victories and breakthroughs, they discover patterns and changing modes. They look at relationships among events. They see some events that caused others to happen. They see events that influenced the group and its work.

Analyzing the turning points

It is here that you ask the group to identify the key turning points, significant changes and shifts in the organization's journey. These points indicate that a significant change has taken place and things in the organization are not the same as they were previously. Each phase can be characterized as a distinct unit within the whole.

FIGURE 18

Vertical lines indicate turning points.

Between them you can name the phases between the turning points.

In the space above the timeline, ask people to mark the key turning points in their history. The conversation helps the group to form a "common mind" and create a larger story about the major phases of their history. Individual stories become part of the common group story. The expenditure of people's energy throughout this particular history becomes meaningful.

Draw vertical lines above the timeline to indicate these points of change in their journey, as seen in Figure 18.

Identifying the key turning points or major historical transitions enables the group to begin to relate to their experience and begin making sense and meaning from it. If posting the events on the wall and stating their reactions to them was about *objectifying* the group's experience, the intent of this step is to *subjectify* it and transform it into a story of their shared experience. Their picture of reality takes on more character as people describe the nature of their experience and explore connections among the various events. Because the group reflects together, they begin constructing their own current understanding of themselves and their given situation. This step is where the group begins to create a narrative or story that explains their situation to themselves.

The result of this step is to give descriptive names to the major phases of the group's history, as in Figure 18. With a brief conversation guide the group to look at each phase. Have them note the

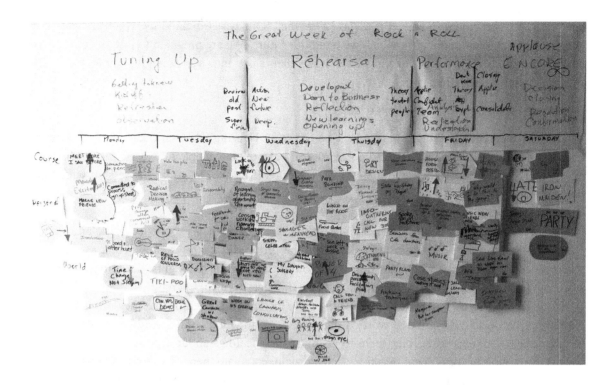

FIGURE 19

This journey wall is complete, with names of phases and the name of the whole time period at the very top.

key events, explain what was happening, recall the mood and pace, and describe the state of the group in that time period. Ask them to give that period a name, like the title of a chapter in a book. In many cases, the group creates a graphic or a poetic image to illustrate each part of the timeline. Images can often express nuances difficult to express in words and help new patterns of meaning to emerge. After they name each of the time periods they identified, ask them to look at the whole timeline and give it a title.

The power of naming

The act of naming enables the group to synthesize what they have discovered about the organization at that time and express it in a short phrase. The name of each phase describes how things were at that given moment and draws their experience into a meaningful narrative. The title for the whole timeline helps the group express a conscious collective relationship to their history, experience and current situation. Titles are often expressed in poetry and metaphor. A simple image like the life cycle of a plant can act as a poetic metaphor giving a group a way to draw their story together as a whole. Their story may be as simple as moving from "baby steps" to "falling down" to "walking confidently" to "taking giant steps." The title for the whole timeline might be something like "determined to be on the move." It is a way of saying, "Our past is behind us. We acknowledge it and see it as the foundation upon which we build our future. We are prepared to face the challenges and opportunities." Their title for the whole draws their story into a meaningful whole. Figure 19 shows a completed timeline.

Decisional Level: Concluding the exercise

The final step enables the group to reflect on the scan. Hearing what various people think helps confirm the group's understanding and consensus and can enable people to express their own commitment. This step re-orients the group toward its future. It brings closure to the session with positive momentum.

Thinking about what happened

Use a brief *focused conversation* to enable the group to reflect on their experience of the process.

Objective questions ask for very tangible things the group did in the exercise, such as the steps taken, words they heard and images they saw. You are asking for highlights, the things that most stood out for them. This part grounds them in the actual details of the exercise.

At the *reflective* level, you might ask for things that made them laugh or that they did not expect. Naming places in the exercise that worried them or where they felt confused and frustrated as well as when they were excited enables them to examine their feelings about aspects of the exercise as well as the group's history. These questions help participants relate themselves to their situation.

The *interpretive* level in this conversation has two aspects. One is discoveries or insights about their situation. Ask the group to share their thoughts about things like greatest accomplishments, greatest challenges, insights into effective strategy, ways to describe the current position, or the impact the group's work has made. You might also include implications that have surfaced for the future.

The choice of questions at this level depends on the focus and rational aims of the journey wall exercise from your preparation. You might ask what trends they can discern from the data, or for a summary of lessons learned. The second question has to do with the effect of the exercise on the group. If, as intended, the exercise has produced new understanding and insight into the group's history and situation, the group itself will have changed, subtly or sometimes even dramatically. They may see mere tendrils of possibility or even state very clear decisions and choices. This level enables the group to look at its own development and give an indication of how they see themselves now.

In this conversation, the *decisional* level gets a light touch. You might ask a quick question, perhaps rhetorical, about how the group will apply its learnings in the future. Or you might ask the group to say how they would describe this exercise to someone who was not present. If they can imagine a professional colleague who deserves a solid, thoughtful answer, their response helps them say something about their relationship to the exercise and their current situation.

Thinking about what happened in the exercise bridges from past to future, from experience to possibility. Each journey wall exercise is unique, with its own specific focus and objectives. It is set in its own context and as part of a larger process. In preparing for the exercise, articulating the rational aim indicates what kind of process to use in this step. See the variations below for options.

Concluding and moving forward

Almost every journey wall exercise closes by clarifying the necessary next steps. Some of these steps will be to document and conclude this step in a larger process and prepare for the next event. Others will relate to actions arising from the exercise and will include assignments and schedules. Still others will have to do with the next gatherings of the group.

This step confirms what the group is resolved to do as a result of the exercise. It grounds the scan exercise in the group's history through tangible actions scheduled on their calendars. It gives the participants a sense that they are engaged in an ongoing process of development and change through their actions. They gain a deeper sense of participating in a positive, purposeful process of organizational evolution.

Practical announcements and a statement of gratitude from the host conclude the journey wall exercise.

Design pattern variations

The journey wall is an extremely flexible way to help any group that wants to take a substantial look at their past. There are myriad specific applications. It is often used to set a contextual backdrop for organizational and strategic planning. It is also used to monitor and guide the implementation of strategies and projects. It is a powerful tool for personal reflection and consciously shaping one's life. The overall methodology and steps are common to all applications, while each exercise is unique and designed for a specific purpose.

Preparation for organizational planning

The journey wall process is often used as an early step in strategic planning, because it provides a platform for envisioning the group's future. For each of the following options you can tailor a process ranging from a couple of reflective questions to a substantial conversation or workshop in itself.

The exercise can focus on monitoring and assessing strategic action. The group looks at their events, achievements, setbacks, tangible results, substantial impact and its significance as well as related happenings in the community, region and world that affect and influence the situation. It can focus on emerging trends, potential barriers and opportunities, strategic position and scenarios for emergent strategy. This step can also be an inquiry into lessons from experience, identifying best practices and designing innovative approaches. The scan can also help a group focus on gaining an understanding of how the organization is performing in relation to its purpose and operational goals.

Reviewing project implementation

A project review looks at actions taken, project events, activities catalyzed by the group's direct action, accomplishments, results and related societal events. To assess the effectiveness of a project or make plans for its future, the question must be broad enough to include the full variety of factors at play. In this case, the scan usually focuses on the actions and accomplishments that happened during the time period under consideration. The process examines challenges and difficulties as well as those factors that are obstructing effective implementation. The scan exercise enables the group to discover the real results and impact they are making. It opens them to discover strategies, actions and activities that will enable them to move forward into a new phase of implementation. It helps them to look at a whole project, assess it and learn from their experience. It launches the group deeper into the cycle of implementing their strategy.

Personal reflection

The journey wall process can also be used for personal reflection on your life and purpose. It will be grounded in the actual events, happenings and marking points in one's life. You can reflect on your personal successes, challenges, insights and purpose. It can help you understand your own history and retell your own life story in a fresh way. As we stand before our experience with honesty and objectivity, we acknowledge our situation and look for ways of using it to move us forward. The scan provides perspectives and reference points that allow us to chart our future direction. Use it a way to keep a journal.

Trend analysis

Looking at the trends emerging in the world and in the field an organization works in can lead to conversations about innovation, possible directions and scenarios for action. Anticipating the future places an organization in a stronger position to respond appropriately as change unfolds in their world.

Strategic thinking

When a group is considering strategies, they often need to gain an understanding of their strategic position. A brainstorm of accomplishments, setbacks, strengths, weaknesses, opportunities and threats as revealed through the journey wall process will provide the basic information for discussion of the strategic state of affairs. The conversation about the relationship between the current situation and the future helps people see their situation and equip them to make strategic and operational choices.

Vision for the future

At any moment, a group has some sense of the future they want to put in place. In a strategic planning retreat, you can position a journey wall exercise before a workshop on the group's vision for the future. A conversation following the scan on future goals, the desired state of the organization in the future, the needs of their constituency and society, opportunities, possibilities and dreams enables the group to express their vision for the future with clarity.

Monitoring strategic implementation

The journey wall can be a powerful tool in monitoring the implementation cycle. It is often used for a six-month or one-year review of the implementation of a strategic initiative or a project. You focus on actions taken, tasks completed and events that have happened in implementing the project. It is important to include events that weren't planned on the timeline, as these often have a significant impact on the results of implementation. The conversation is primarily to understand what has happened, the current position of each element, successes, challenges and next steps for project action.

Project assessment

If the journey wall is focused on assessing or evaluating an initiative, the group will look at things like their achievements, the actual results, the impact of their work and its significance. They will place their emphasis on gaining a grounded picture of what has happened, the changes that have taken place and the relationship to the organization's goals. They will examine the effects of their work and seek ways of understanding its importance. This is a very powerful way to do a "lessons learned" exercise, because it is based on the whole journey of the project.

Organizational learning

A journey wall is also a strong developmental tool. If the group is trying to learn how to be most effective as a group, they will focus on the specific lessons they can draw from their experience, insights into best practices, and innovative approaches. They will look back at specific events or time periods or patterns that are revealed over time. They will look at how they did things, who was involved and what happened. They will find their mistakes and be able to assess their capacity objectively. They will devise alterative strategies and new approaches to their projects and tasks.

Impact of the journey wall

The journey wall can have an outsized impact when used with groups. The following are just three examples of the difference it made in specific settings.

Healing a communication breakdown

One elderly couple, married for many years, were not speaking to each other after a painful incident. When one of their children presented them with a journey wall of their family, they looked back at all the ups and downs of their life together, and the longer timeline of their relationship helped them see their recent troubles in perspective, and they began communicating with each other again.

Gaining perspective on traumatic history

A young Indigenous woman, translating a just-created 200-year journey wall back into her ancestral language for the elders to understand, suddenly stopped in the middle in astonishment. She had just articulated events such as the smallpox epidemic that nearly wiped out the whole population, the residential schools and the 60s scoop of children from their families that cut off the transmission of culture and values. She suddenly exclaimed in English, "We've been through all that and we are still here? We are one helluva people!" Her anger at the outside world changed and her life work became focused on strengthening her culture and the environment around her land.

Transcending a bad merger experience

Two service organizations had been forced to merge to maintain their government funding. The smaller of the two, which had a more collegial and relaxed structure, absorbed the larger, more hierarchical organization. Five years after the merger, they were still at odds with each other. They did a journey wall going back 10 years, to include the events and accomplishments of both original organizations and the events of the merger itself. It emerged during the posting of events that some people had literally moved into broom closets to make room for the new people. When the group shared this information, they began to forgive themselves and each other for the past and went on to create a vibrant shared vision together.

Conclusion

The act of creating a journey wall can heal individuals and groups, and provide a grounded standpoint for creating the future.

Practical resources

ICA Associates Inc. has created a small handbook for facilitating the journey wall, available through the ICA Associates office.[65]

---

65 http://www.ica-associates.ca/

Section 3   ToP Facilitation Design

Three simple ideas—description, phenomenon, intentionality—
provided enough inspiration to keep roomfuls of Husserlian
assistants busy in Freiburg for decades. With all of human existence
awaiting their attention, how could they ever run out of things to do?
                                          —Sarah Bakewell[66]

66 Bakewell, 2016, p. 46

10.
The ToP Design Eye

We did not put our ideas together. We put our purposes together. And we agreed, and then we decided.

—Popol Vuh[67]

A client called, wanting some facilitation help in making some cultural changes in her community foundation. Another facilitator had come to facilitate a ToP strategic planning process, but had just done it "by the book" without asking many questions of her or the group in preparation, and the planning process had missed the mark so badly that nobody wanted to do something like that again. We talked several times about what she needed, and it was still unclear. She was herself a trained facilitator, and she'd already tried many techniques to deal with the challenges her foundation was facing.

So we started by facilitating an exercise with the *organizational journey map*[68] (see Figure 43 on page 188) with the staff and board as a diagnostic tool to determine the current and preferred culture of the organization, which gave us some insights into their struggles and aspirations. After extensive discussion about her underlying intent for a facilitated "retreat day" with the board and staff, we talked through the product and the experience the group needed, the contradictions they were struggling with, and the images in the group that needed to change. Then we designed the process to accomplish those needs.

Since she wanted the staff to understand the community impact that their mundane work was having, and to experience the joy of coming to work, we started the retreat with a storytelling exercise to share stories of impact. There were spontaneous outbursts of astonishment and pride at the stories. Then people wrote narratives of what they wanted the organization to look like based on

67 From the *Popol Vuh*, the sacred Book of the People of the K'iche' of Guatemala, as quoted in Kahane, 2017

68 Stanfield, 1997

their journey map analysis, identified underlying obstacles to that vision, and brainstormed a list of practical actions to address the obstacles and bring the culture they wanted into being. In the final evaluation conversation, they articulated their pride in working for an organization with such powerful impact, and committed to the cultural changes, such as improved internal communication. The careful attention to the design of the event helped the group attain its aims.

Background

The Technology of Participation, in all its applications, is characterized by methodological consistency. Not only does the phenomenological method underlie all ToP tools and the way they are used, but it also forms the very structure of the design process itself. The phenomenological method is key to listening to the client, designing the steps of the process, choosing the appropriate tools, and facilitating the whole event. In this sense, moving from careful attention to the client's input, through process design, to getting the results the group needs is a holistic journey.

Beatrice Briggs, a facilitator colleague in Mexico, created a video where she describes the role of the facilitator as architect, pilot and guide.[69] So far this book has explored the pilot and guide roles extensively. As an architect the facilitator uses a design process to plan the steps that the group will go through. The facilitator's design role as the architect of process is often overlooked. But it is crucial to ensuring that not only that the intervention accomplishes the needed results, but also that the needed transformation of the group happens so that those results have their most powerful impact.

Design as art and science

ToP facilitation design is a disciplined process used to develop innovative, high-quality facilitation plans for collaborative group work. Its *intentional focus* is build the design for a facilitated process on the real needs of the client. The facilitator calls upon information, experience, knowledge and intuition to create, shape and refine the processes to bring out the greatest meaning and best possible results for each unique situation.

Phenomenological inquiry

ToP methodology provides us with a *method of inquiry* for collaboration, a clear journey from conception to completion and reflection. As with all phenomenological inquiries, the design process begins with gathering the most basic information about the client, their situation and their objectives. It includes subjective reflections about the nature of the inquiry, the dynamics of the group and its culture. It brings this information together to identify the key factors, determine objectives and articulate critical questions. All that information in turn becomes the starting point to create a facilitation plan for that situation, after which the facilitator recalls previous similar experiences, explores possible techniques to use, and decides on the specific facilitation plan for this situation.

---

69 IIFAC video, 2013

Neutrality begins with design

In designing facilitation processes, the intentional focus is firmly fixed on the group. Before anything, it is critical that you set aside all assumptions, judgments, theories, presuppositions, beliefs, ready-made or pre-fabricated interpretations and possible solutions to be able to focus on the object of the inquiry itself without interference. This temporary suspension of all external beliefs places the focus solely on the inquiry itself. This attitude creates the conditions of *radical openness* within which an authentic inquiry can take place. Husserl called it *bracketing* to indicate that while certain thoughts and ideas may arise in our minds, if we are to engage in this kind of inquiry, we must set them aside. When we are able to do that, we are ready to begin listening to the group. If we are not able to assume that posture, we are really listening to ourselves rather than the client.

Facilitator neutrality is essential even before meeting or speaking with the person requesting the intervention. This internal discipline becomes more like the condition of your skin than a coat you wear or a checklist to complete. ToP facilitators approach each prospective project with a blank slate—tabula rasa—the only thing present is pure, open possibility. The situation must speak for itself. ToP facilitators avoid making guesses at the "real problem." There are no ready-made opportunities to use a favorite process or tool, no places for the facilitator to influence some social issue—nothing but the client and open possibility. Indeed, in some cases ToP facilitation may not be the necessary approach. Adopting the phenomenological attitude itself is what provides the way for us to neutrally design a process and maintain an open stance to possible options through the entire engagement.

Reverse engineering:
Working backward from the needed results to discern stages of understanding and consensus

The actual design process begins at the end. The focus is on the product and results of the process. That "tangible thing" becomes the reference point for the whole process.

Once you know the type of product or result, the question you must ask is, "What stages or platforms of understanding must the group reach in order to achieve those results?" For example, if a group is building a model for a new program or service, they will craft a specific model out of elements that meet agreed-upon criteria and advance the organization's purpose.

There are several levels of understanding in that simple thought. Figure 20 illustrates the levels of understanding, building up from the bottom left like stairs.

Each stage is a platform enabling the group to move to the next stage. Successful groups go through a thinking journey to a shared understanding. When the situation and context are clear, the group can begin to envision appropriate elements and images of what they're trying to build. They can assess the appropriateness and innovative quality of their ideas by establishing values or criteria that clarify priorities and strategic advantages. They can weave the various elements together into a coherent plan or model that will move them strategically forward.

The key to the group's success is for you as the facilitator is to map out the necessary incremental thinking processes and find the major stages of understanding that they must navigate. Finding

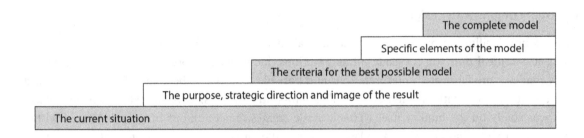

FIGURE 20

Stages or platforms of understanding the facilitator must reach to create a successful design

these stages or platforms enables you to sketch out broad images of the process and then to create detailed procedures to create a meaningful event.

To find the stages of understanding so you can plan the process, start at the result and move incrementally backward (from the top step at the right to the lower steps at the left in this diagram), asking what the group needs to know in order to get to each stage in turn.

To get to the result of the steps in the example on the steps above, the facilitator asks "What results are needed at each step?" to discern the stages of thinking.

For example:

.... To get the complete model, the group must identify the major aspects of the program.

.... To get the major aspects of the program model, the group must identify specific elements to include in the model.

.... To get specific elements that are appropriate and will lead to success, the group must relate to a set of common criteria and values.

................To get a clear sense of the criteria for the best possible model, the group must have a common sense of the purpose, strategic direction and image of the result and an understanding of the current situation.

As the stages of understanding become clear, you can begin to tailor group activity and facilitation processes that will enable purposeful collaborative inquiry for the specific situation.

Now you can move forward, starting with the bottom step. Following the same example:

.... An understanding of the current situation and the purpose, strategic direction and image of the result might involve activities such as presentations, group conversations, a journey wall, or an analysis of the need for a solution, that help the participants gain a common understanding of the foundations of the inquiry.

.... Gaining a clear sense of the criteria for the best model possible might require brainstorming, clustering and even prioritizing principles, values and criteria to use in shaping the model and making choices about it. It may involve additional context and reflections on purpose, strategy, and ethics. In a complex process, it could take place in stages.

.... Identifying specific elements may involve multiple forms of research and group brainstorming. Depending on the complexity of the model itself, there could be several topics, such as program objectives, major content, structure, roles and accountability relationships.

................Finalizing the major aspects of the program might involve activities such as clustering ideas to determine program objectives, creating relationship and structure maps, clarifying roles and outlining key policies and procedures. As the whole picture comes together, a whole model is formed.

Artistry

Design as an art has to do with using intuition, knowledge and experience in solving design problems and conceptualizing appropriate solutions. It involves playing with thoughts, ideas and possibilities in a creative process.

The artistic design process begins with a style of being totally relaxed and flexible with models and constructs. You set aside your assumptions and preferences to listen. Questions tease out information, reflections, ideas and conclusions. Careful, intuitive listening helps you pick up on bits of implicit information and connections among various elements that don't always seem to be significant. As connections, explanations and solutions pop up, note them as information. Each idea helps you weave a fuller understanding of the situation. Because ToP facilitators are often called on to address complex situations, exploring related ideas and aspects can reveal more of the situation's depth and texture. As you seek connections some will reveal a pattern that might enable the group. As your exploration evolves, appropriate meta-models and a complex of elements will become clear enough to test and use in your approach.

Another part of the artistry is in weaving complex factors into a meta-model and a complex of questions and activities that can address the needs of the situation. You might need to map the complexity to create an understanding of the relationships and dynamics within the content. Take into account the stages of understanding that a group goes through while fitting the pieces together and evolving a consensus. The artistry is creating all of the lines of music, the details that create the drama and harmony of a symphony.

The artistry in the design ensures that your event is based on respect and honouring the clarity and wisdom of the group. The atmosphere and context create an atmosphere of welcome. The activity is engaging and stimulates high quality collaboration through engaging multiple ways of processing information and ease of participation. Recording responses in their original words highlights respect for the group.

An artful design integrates the insights of the facilitator, using intuition that is built on a substantial body of real experience. That experience might come from other methodologies and approaches, similar problems you've seen, and and things you've tried from the past.

A profound design addresses deep human questions and foundational images that people are operating from. The design allows the participants to acknowledge the interior crisis and existential questions in their real situation, the awareness of an urge to escape their situation, and enables

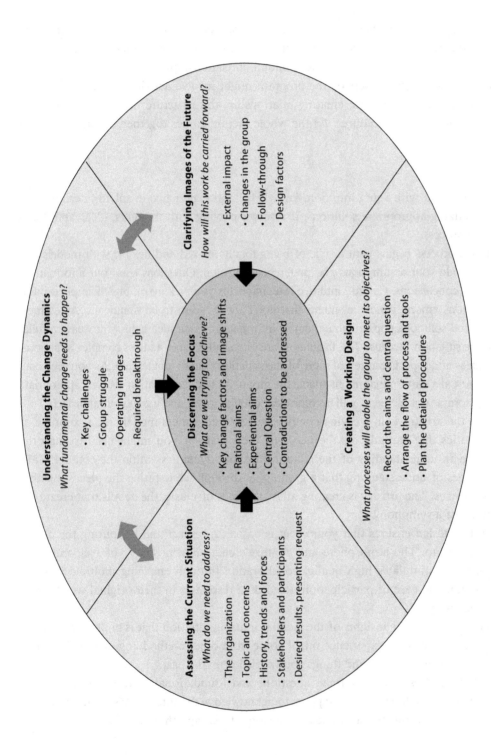

FIGURE 21

The ToP "design eye." Notice the arrows in the visual showing the flow of information and how each part affects the whole process.

authentic responses. The images of individuals and the group are shifted in alignment with existential breakthrough and self-understanding.

The ToP "Design Eye": Five steps in ToP facilitation design

The format of this design process is a relatively recent creation, based on the phenomenological method described in this book and ICA's many-faceted work with designing processes over 50 years. You can use it to design a detailed plan for complex events that are more than one session, or for complicated topics that require deep inquiry in order to understand enough to create an appropriate process. A facilitator colleague, Jerry Mings, dubbed the format, seen in Figure 21, the "design eye."

In a global sense, the ToP facilitation design process covers two main dimensions. *Listening to your client* is where you develop a deep understanding of the situation: its structure, history, systems, people, conundrums and desires. You ask the client questions to understand what is going on and what they need. *Designing the process* is where you develop facilitation processes that enable the group to achieve its objectives, build consensus and deepen commitment. This part goes beyond what the client has said, requiring care-filled discernment.

Listening to your client
1. Assessing the current situation: What does this process need to address?
2. Understanding the change dynamics: What change needs to happen?
3. Clarifying images of the future: How will this work be carried forward?

Designing the process
4. Discerning the focus: What are we trying to achieve?
5. Creating a working design: What processes will enable this group to meet its objectives?

This section provides a comprehensive list of the areas where the facilitator needs to understand the client, and the kind of questions to ask for each area. It is rarely necessary to ask every single question. For ease of use, each step starts with a checklist.

1. Assessing the current situation

- The organization
- Topic and current concerns
- History, trends and forces
- Stakeholders and participants
- Desired results or the presenting request from the client

The organization

The first step is to gain an overall image of the organization, so you have the widest context possible. In some cases, information about the whole organization is necessary. In some, it is enough to understand the part of the organization that you'll be working with, such as a department. Depending on the situation, this step can be rather quick and impressionistic, preparing you to locate the event in the specific organizational context.

- Describe the organization.
- What does the organization do?
- What is your mission and purpose?
- How many employees?

Topic and current concerns

It is important to identify the specific topic of the event as objectively as possible. While every topic is complex, it is necessary to say what this event is about in a clear way that focuses and delimits the main topic of the event. You want to identify the topics people are discussing in this area and the concerns they feel need to be addressed. You are also getting information about the depth of concern and the flavour of the current situation. This data helps you to establish and maintain a focus on the most relevant topic.

- What is the event to be about?
- What is the major topic?
- What are people's concerns in this area?
- What related "issues" are people raising?
- What concerns evoke the most passion?
- Where do people seem "stuck" in relation to this topic?
- What are the key questions that need to be addressed in this area?

History, trends and forces

There is history around the main topic, and you need to understand the trends and forces that are affecting the direction of that main topic. You want to gain a sense of what has happened in this area. Knowledge of the organization's history will provide clues to the events as well as the forces acting on the organization. You also want to get a feeling for directions emerging in the larger field and in the organization.

- What have been the greatest accomplishments in this area?
- What have been the most significant setbacks in this area?
- What are the key events that have brought you to think of this kind of event?
- What, outside the organization, is affecting or influencing this area?
- What is happening inside the organization that is influencing your situation?
- What trends, innovations and new directions are emerging in your field?
- When have you worked on this topic before?
- What work has already been done on this issue?

Stakeholders and participants

Identifying the stakeholders will help you understand the relationships in the group. It illuminates the spectrum of perspectives that need to be heard. It is best to identify distinct groups of stakeholders. Those who are involved and affected most directly will be the most likely participants in the processes you design.

- Who will be affected directly? Who more indirectly?
- Who has information and perspectives that need to be included?

- Who will implement the results?
- Who needs to participate in the events?

Desired results

You're trying to understand what tangible results are needed from the facilitated process. What the organization needs from the process depends on the topic and the key concerns. You will need to know what direct results or products the organization wants. It is also important to gain a solid idea of the impact the organization wants to make in its sphere of influence, beyond the presenting issue. It is important for the results and products to be described as concretely as possible—even to the point of who will implement the outcomes—to the extent of talking to those people to see what they need.

- What results do you need from this project?
- Are there decisions to be made?
- What kinds of "products" do you need from this event?

2. Understanding the change dynamics

- Key challenges
- Group struggle
- Operating images
- Required breakthrough

Key challenges

Finding and identifying the major challenges helps you design activities, conversations and work sessions. In many cases, these issues are deep, long-term, systemic factors and key elements of the organization's culture. If a ToP event is to be able to help the organization move forward, you must find ways to enable the group to address the core challenges to success.

- What nagging issues plague the organization?
- Where is the group most challenged?
- What are the greatest barriers to success?
- Looking long term, what are the two to three most strategic issues that must be addressed in order for the group to move forward?

Group struggle

Examining the group's deep struggles enables you to discover where the people in the organization are raising the deepest questions. These will often be areas of the greatest ambiguity, or where people are in a state of misalignment with some dimension of the organization, its direction and how it operates. You are seeking an understanding of the most primal, existential questions being raised in the situation.

- Where does the group struggle?
- What topic or concerns are most difficult?
- What items have been 'undiscussable'?
- What deeper, pressing questions are being raised?

Operating images

It is critical to gain an understanding of the people and their relationship to the topic. Discussions in this area will focus on the people in the organization and its culture, including how the group sees itself in relation to the whole organization, how teams operate internally and with each other, how they work out issues, and generally how they perceive the world. It is necessary to gain a sense of things in this area so you can engage people appropriately and guide the conversations successfully.

- What is expected of the participants?
- What is their role in making choices and decisions?
- How much knowledge and capacity is present in the group?
- How successful has the group been in dealing with this topic?
- What is the current mood of the group in relation to this topic?
- What is the current level of consensus over the topic?
- What are the keys to the way the group operates?
- How does the group see itself within the whole organization?

Required breakthrough

After discussing the key challenges, struggles and images of the group, asking the client to articulate the breakthrough that they desire will catalyze positive thinking about what will be required for the intervention to be a success. You are now asking the client to extrapolate what a meaningful result looks like, based on all the data and intuition they have shared in the conversation to this point.

- What would a successful result of this event look like?
- How does this group need to be different at the end of the event?
- What breakthrough would fundamentally change the organization in a positive way?

3. Clarifying images of the future

- External impact
- Changes in the group
- Follow-through
- Design factors

External impact

In this stage you are asking the client to articulate the larger context of the results of the event. Effort here helps ensure that the results can be used or implemented effectively. The client is moving their thinking beyond the present data to explore the future.

- What things going on in the larger world will affect the results of our work?
- Describe the possible impact of this project beyond the organization itself.
- What difference will this make?
- What real shifts seem to be necessary?
- What results will be necessary from our work together?

Changes in the group

It is wise to begin discussions about what kinds of changes the organization needs before the event. Having a real sense of how the people relate to the focus of the project enables you to help the group make choices about how they approach their situation. This consideration is the future aspect of the work you did on group struggle and operating images in the previous section. These questions will help in expressing the experiential aim.

- What critical questions are the people and the organization facing?
- How will this work impact the culture of the organization?
- How do the people in the group relate to their task?
- What shifts in culture may be needed?
- How do the participants need to be different as a result of our work together?

Follow-through

Knowing how the results will be implemented will help shape the design. Sometimes organizational structures and systems will be the primary vehicle, while other times, results may be carried out by task forces that form in relation to common interests. Sometimes the deliberations or recommendations are a product that will inform action by other people such as management or a government body. Sometimes the client might need to develop an understanding of formal decision-making requirements and necessary protocols as well as ongoing coordination of implementation.

- Who will carry out any plans made during this event?
- How will the results be used?
- How will task assignments be made?
- What organizations, groups, teams, departments, and so on will be involved in the implementation?
- What approval or ratification is necessary?
- Who is finally responsible for this?
- How will the effort be coordinated?
- How will decisions be made?
- How will monitoring and accountability happen?

Design factors

In the initial conversations it is important to clarify any parameters that will affect the work. This is the moment to begin discussing time, space, budget and arrangements. Knowing what time can be made available is critical. The process must be able to accomplish the objectives within the given time. There is often need for dialogue with groups in order to ensure adequate time is available. In some cases, it may be necessary to adjust aims and expectations in relation to available time and people. Sometimes other related topics must be dealt with at the same time as the focus topic. Discussions about space, technology and arrangements begin here simply to gain a comprehensive sense of what will be required. Budgeting must fit the whole project and is another factor in the elasticity of the design parameters.

- What time is available for this project?
- Who will be participating?
- Where will the events be held?
- What logistical arrangements need to be made and who is responsible?
- What is the budget for this project?
- What technology is available or required?
- What inputs or preparation will need to be done ahead of time?
- What form of documentation or reports will be needed?
- Is there anything we have forgotten to mention?

Up to this point, the facilitator's role in process design has been to listen carefully and dispassionately, assembling all the information that the client can provide as the building blocks to process.

4. Discerning the focus

Now we move to the centre or the iris of the "design eye." At this point there is a subtle shift in role from listener to analyst. It can be in dialogue with client, but your analytical skills come more into play here as you push for more depth and synthesis.

Perhaps the most critical part of preparing for a facilitated event is articulating the objectives. Here is where what I call *reverse engineering* comes into play, beginning from the end and working backwards. Of course, after you think everything through from the end of the event, you also have to go through the plans from the beginning to the end to ensure that there is consistency and continuity of thought throughout the event. You want to ensure that the sequence will guide the group through appropriate levels of thought to achieve their desired objectives. As the facilitator who is bringing objectivity to the analysis of the data gathered in stages 1-3, you lead this stage, although you often also talk this stage through with the client. Your expertise in process and detachment from the content are useful in going beneath the surface to discern the underlying focus, while the client's full knowledge of the situation keeps the focus grounded.

- Key change factors and image shifts
- Rational aims
- Experiential aims
- Central question
- Contradictions to be addressed

Key change factors and image shifts

First and most critical is the topic and the key concerns related to it. The specific concerns illuminate the nature of the topic and therefore help you find the focus of the inquiry. The desired results and impact must be sharpened and made as specific as possible. It is critical to identify the key challenges and contradictions[70] the group is facing as well as their relationship to the situation and the project. The time frame related to the topic itself will indicate the scope and depth of the inquiry.

---

70 See page 70 for a discussion of contradictions.

The time that can be dedicated to this inquiry will affect the work that can be successfully done by a group. You also need to know who will actually participate.

- What innovations or perhaps odd or wild suggestions or changes are being expressed?
- What are the underlying images that the group is operating from, and what images would help them move forward?
- What real shifts seem to be necessary?

Rational aims

The rational aim is the practical goal of the event, a succinct articulation of the desired result. The aim could be a product such as the key elements of a group's shared vision. It could be a decision about which photocopier to buy. It could be a solution to a problem like addressing absenteeism. It could be the key life insights gained from watching a movie. In any case it will articulate the specific results the group wants to achieve in relation to the topic during the session.

If complex engagement involves several events, the overall rational aim will focus on the end result. For example, a strategic plan might involve many specific facilitated events conducted over several weeks or months. The rational aim for the whole process will be stated at the highest level; something like "A set of coordinated strategic action campaigns to extend our impact will be ready for immediate implementation."

The rational aim tells you the kind of result required by the event or engagement. It's clear and unambiguous, but it says nothing about the actual content of the results. The aims of a facilitated event are always stated in relationship to a specific topic. In the example in the last paragraph, the specific topic is strategic action.

The rational aim clearly delimits the scope of the event. This is one of the key principles of phenomenological inquiry. The focus says this discussion is about this thing and not other things. It isolates a topic within in its environment and places it in the light for inquiry. The rational aim names the topic as well as the kind of outcome required. It says, for example, that this event needs to enable the group to assess the implications of a review of its service to customers. The event would only include things like product design or marketing strategies inasmuch as they are clearly related to the review of customer service. This aim indicates that this event will not even attempt to offer solutions. It will focus entirely on the review and analysis. Solutions will require a different event, after the implications of the review sink in.

The rational aim provides an overall reference point and a steering rudder for the event. It guides your preparation and planning. In most cases, the rational aim will provide a way to determine the most important interpretive or decisional level question. For example, the key interpretive question in a conversation about implications will be something like "What are the key implications that must be addressed in order to improve customer service?" Depending on the requirements of the situation, the implications might need to be prioritized, but the key question for the group's work has to do with stating implications. Knowing this, you can then back your way through a series of questions that prepare the group to respond to that question.

The rational aim also helps you make decisions during the event. For example, if members of the group find a side topic particularly fascinating, the rational aim allows you to gently remind the group of the intent of the meeting and ask them if they want to continue on the new topic or put it aside for another meeting. It enables you to keep the conversation on track and helps you manage time. If the group launches into a long discussion of their feelings about the review or its methodology and it appears they won't have time to complete a substantial discussion of implications, you can help them process those feelings quickly and ask them to bring that question to a close and take the next step toward its goal.

- What does the group need to understand by the end of this event?
- What specific results are necessary?
- What concrete products do we need to create?
- What are the outcomes we need to see?

Existential aims

The existential aim (sometimes called experiential aim) enables the group to make fully conscious choices about how they relate to their given topic. It's about the relationship individuals and groups take to their situation, the topic and the question. From the same root as the word "existence", the existential aim is about how participants "be different" at the end of the session. It is about their image of themselves in relation to their situation that matters. It is about the way the event addresses the group and the way they relate to that address. If the rational aim is seen as the external aspect of the session, the existential aim is more focused on the internal, personal aspect.

We often use the phrase, "How does the group need to be different at the close of the session?" It is not a description of the quality of the event or the experience the participants have during the event. Nor does it have to do with whether they enjoyed the session or liked the discussion or loved the facilitator or whether they had fun and felt good about each other. All of those factors contribute to a successful event, but the key question is how does the group relate to their own situation.

What matters is how they have given real shape and texture to their relationship to the situation and the topic. A complex, difficult discussion with multiple perspectives that are strongly held and fiercely debated can elicit a way of being that is quite appropriate and helpful to the group. It might not be entirely pleasant to get to the bottom of disagreements, but it might be necessary if the existential objective is to form a common mind about something.

Suppose the group needs to develop a strategic action plan for recruiting new staff to ensure a successful leadership succession and the very sustainability of the organization. The experiential aim may have to do with getting a firm consensus and genuine commitment to the plan. They began with no plan, just a situation and a question. They finish the workshop with a clear plan and a real willingness to move forward together to achieve it. In this case the act of investing one's ideas and thinking together builds consensus and commitment. The group may not be aware or be able to say that their deepest questions have been resolved, but they certainly will feel it as well as understand what they have created a plan that they feel compelled to act on.

Because the aims, topics, people and time available for each event are unique, each experiential aim is also unique. Your question, with those who determine the overall objectives of the event, is something like, "Given this topic, these concerns, these people, this rational objective and the time we have for this event, how do we want this group to be different at the end of the session?"

Central question

The central focus question states the central question for the group to address. It is a practical question that identifies the topic and asks a question the participants can respond to creatively and strategically. The central focus question is "the thing itself," as Edmund Husserl used the term, in that it grounds the inquiry in the reality of the organization's field of concern and development. It is toward that question that participants direct their consciousness. It becomes the fixed pivot point for preparing and conducting the whole inquiry.

It is here where you clarify the primary question to be resolved by the group. It has always been true that everything in our world is related and connected. If the focus of a project or event is vague, the group will, quite naturally, explore all of its aspects of it and all related questions, getting way off track. Often this results in discussions that are only tangentially related to the intended focus, frustrating others so they complain of irrelevant conversation and feel their time has been wasted.

One of the tasks of a central question, then, is to delimit the conversation in order to focus on what is intended and have more productive discussions. The central question must state the topic clearly and ask the question that the group needs to answer. A good, clear focus question will trigger reflection in the participants and enable them to respond to it with appropriate answers.

- What is the central question, that, when we answer it in this session, will create the results that are needed?

Contradictions to be addressed

At this stage, you are discerning what is blocking breakthrough in the group. If a ToP event is to help the organization move forward, the facilitator must find ways to enable the group to address the core challenges to success. Addressing the underlying contradiction that is holding a group back will make transformation possible. Earlier discussion of struggles, challenges, and possible break-through are some of the indicators that lead to this analysis. (For more about underlying contradictions, see pages 70-71.)

- What are the underlying contradictions that are preventing the group from moving forward?
- What might be the doorway to the future that the group needs to discern?

5. Creating a working design

At this point as the facilitator or consultant you are working on your own or with your team to take all the information that you gathered and work through the design. This is the first time you take the brackets off considering what you will actually do. Only now do you switch roles from listener and analyst to designer. Use these steps to plan:

- Record the aims and central question
- Arrange the flow of process and tools
- Plan the detailed procedures
- If the consultation will be complex, create a simple design map

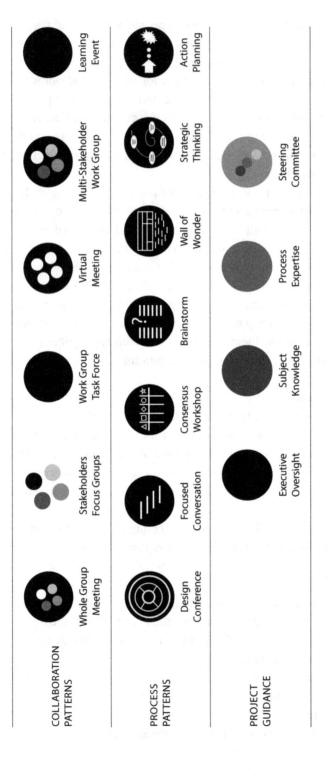

FIGURE 22

The key to the design images for use in a design map

Record the aims and central question

In this step you define the tangible results and what the human change will actually look like. You identify the necessary results, decisions and elements of a solution. Clarifying the human change involves stating the intended change in the images a group is operating from, the formation of a common will, consensus development and the commitment to move forward. The aims have been articulated in the analysis in the last step above, so these questions allow a second look and may go deeper.

- What type of solution or result is the organization asking for? They might want a model, a plan, or something else.
- What decisions and tangible products are required?
- What contradictions and existential question must be addressed?
- What images must shift or change?
- What common will and personal commitments are needed?

Arrange the flow of process and tools

a. First, identify the major stages of the process

This step involves outlining the key questions, breakthroughs and major working topics for the event. It also must describe the main stages or platforms of understanding leading to fulfillment of the aims and objectives. It will help you determine the major steps to take in the process of the event.

- What key questions must the group address?
- What is the breakthrough needed?
- What must be understood, resolved or created before reaching the result?
- What major questions will be needed to reach those understandings?
- What connections, relationships, experiences and feelings must be surfaced?
- What basic information will be needed to address this topic?
- What major group work items are needed?
- Describe the thinking steps needed.

b. Then, discern the process flow

This step involves creating your design map for the event. It places the topics and major stages for group work in a practical time frame. It creates a logical flow of thinking stages and identifies the methodology appropriate for each step and for the whole event. It holds the journey that the group needs to take to accomplish the aims.

- Develop a logical flow for the overall event.
- Look for cognitive processing models appropriate to the given situation.
- Create a design map that shows the major methodological steps.

Plan the detailed procedures

Refine the model by fleshing out the procedural steps and determining the appropriate atmosphere for the event.

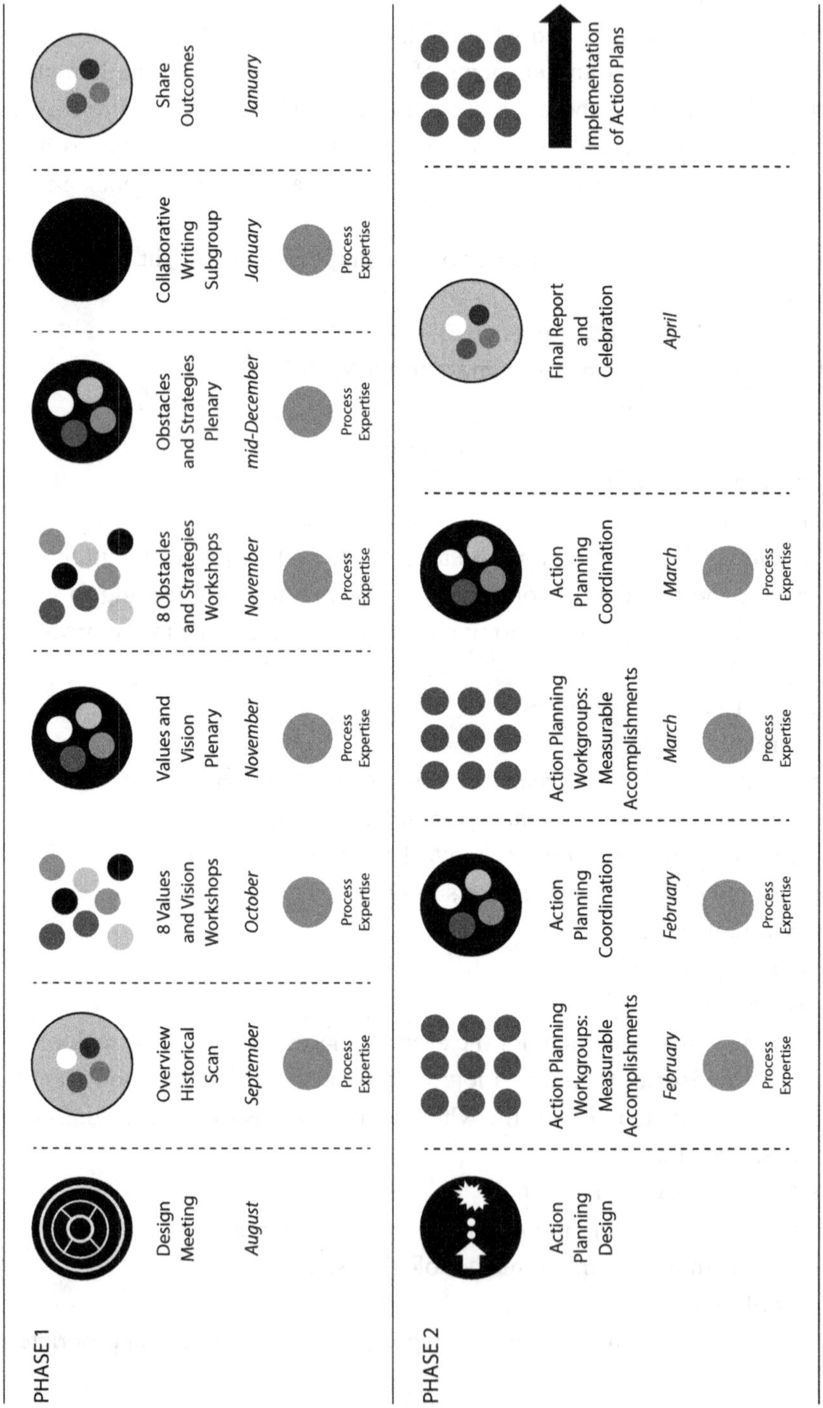

FIGURE 23

The actual design map used for a complex planning process. For a key to the symbols, see Figure 22.

Write the script or the notes that you will use to guide the group. Include the precise steps you will ask the group to take, the timing for each section, and list the materials you will need at each step.

Finally, rehearse the design as if you are doing it, either in your own head or with a colleague. If any doubts or fuzziness arise in your mind about how it will work, resolve them before the event.

You can find a worksheet that might help you create your design in the appendix on page 185.

Create a simple design map

Your client does not usually need to see your detailed procedures, but they might need a way to visualize where the process is going and a way to communicate the flow with their group. In complex interventions with many different meetings with different groups, a visual design map can portray the whole intervention in a graphical format that shows the whole design in symbols or images. This picture helps the client and participants easily grasp and remember the flow of the events and parts of the process.

Inspired by a presentation on *collaborative architecture* by Sam Kaner[71], the following design image is intended to represent different ToP elements simply. The images show collaboration patterns, the ways participants will work together at different stages of the process, and process patterns, the tools or processes that the facilitator will bring to the group.

Put the collaboration patterns in one row to show the events on a timeline.

Put the process patterns under the symbol for the event.

Put the necessary guidance events along the timeline.

Add annotations to describe the overall process design.

Figure 22 shows some visual symbols for a design map, followed in Figure 23 by an actual design map that was used to help a client.

Conclusion

The ToP design process works because it follows the phenomenological process: first get clear objectively and on what is going on in the client situation and the internal responses of the group and yourself, then analyze the deeper meaning of the situation, and finally design a solution. Following these steps ensures that the process will achieve what the client needs.

---

71 Kaner, Sam, "Participatory Decision-Making in Multi-Stakeholder Collaboration" http://chl. berkeley.edu/images/stories/conference/kaner.pdf

Section 4 Study Methodologies

The point is to keep coming back to the "things themselves"—phenomena stripped of their conceptual baggage—so as to bail out weak or extraneous material and get to the heart of the experience . . . . It restores this personal world in its richness, arranged around our own perspective yet usually no more noticed than the air.

—Sarah Bakewell[72]

72 Bakewell, 2016, page 43

The charting and seminar methods

If you've seen a group spend valuable meeting time pooling their ignorance of a topic, then you understand that often a group needs to understand a policy paper, or a context laid out in a document or book, before they can work together to create solutions or reach decisions. It is usually not enough to ask people to read the material before they arrive at a meeting—few people have or will take the time. Methods that help individuals or groups to quickly and efficiently gain new or foundational knowledge before they begin to work creatively as a group help the facilitator guide the group to wise decisions. The charting and seminar methods in this section, though not strictly facilitation methods, work well with other ToP facilitation tools, as they are based on the same underlying thought patterns.

Long before facilitation became a focus of ICA's work, let alone a profession, Institute staff developed and practiced intellectual and study methods based on phenomenology. The methods were designed to help individuals deeply understand the contents of a book or paper, come to significant insights, and apply them to their own lives and work. Trainers used them in powerful weekend seminars that had deep impact on participants' lives. These methods are foundational ICA methods that apply the phenomenological method. They are still used in training, of course, but now they have become valuable tools for groups to understand printed materials as a foundation for building consensus. The charting method also became applied to time, and is a foundation for the journey wall method.

11.
Charting

You are not interested in ideas, but in the human being that is over against you in this. You are interested in the self. You have not charted unless you are other than what you were when you began. You may have gone through some intellectual rational process, but you have not charted. Charting is changing your posture and your being in history. Or to put it another way, it is the gimmick whereby you alter your existence through the genuine encounter with another human being.

—Joseph Mathews[73]

In my last year of university, I put one assignment off until the very last moment. I needed to read a book of essays, then summarize five of them. I had only one day to read the whole book and finish the assignment, and my graduation depended on it. Suddenly I remembered that I had learned the charting method in a course with the Institute. I quickly made a high level chart of the whole book, making a visual chart to get a sense of the flow of the essays and the likely content. From that chart, I chose the five essays that interested me most to work on. I quickly charted each of these, using structural clues to find the core content and summarize it on a visual chart. Then I wrote a paragraph that reflected the key points in each essay. The paper was finished in less than a day, leaving me time to type it up and hand it in before the deadline.

Years later, after becoming a facilitator, I participated in a two-day training session for community facilitators in order to qualify for a chance for a contract with a government agency. The professor who had designed the process presented us each with a four-inch thick manual, and proceeded to walk us through it, word for word, page by page. The experienced facilitators in the room quickly lost interest, became resentful, and checked out. In order to understand the big picture of what would be required of us, I took out a sheet of paper and made a visual chart of the whole manual instead of listening to the presenter. That evening I copied my handwritten chart and offered the

---

73 Mathews, 1968

copies to everyone in the room, as a way to get a handle on the big picture. Even the presenter was grateful to see each of the pieces of the manual in relation to the whole project.

Background

We often feel that by reading something we will absorb the content. In "How to Read a Book"[74], Mortimer J. Adler and Charles Van Doren describe four levels of reading.

1. Elementary reading, which involves basic reading skills like vocabulary and grammar. At this level, we become literate; so we can understand what is being said.
2. Inspectional reading, which they describe as "skimming systematically." It is a very quick look in order to gain an overview.
3. Analytical reading is reading in depth for the sake of understanding.
4. Syntopical reading or comparative reading in which the reader seeks to analyze a topic through the reading and analysis of several works.

Charting was developed primarily from levels two and three. The method begins with their level two, skimming the given work and highlighting key words, phrases and ideas. In their section on analytical reading, Adler and Van Doren advocate creating an outline of a book. Their examples of outlines follow the traditional, vertical format. ICA devised a way to hold the whole picture and the details at the same time in a horizontal picture.

Figure 25 shows a topical chart of Chapter 7 in *The Courage to Lead*, by Brian Stanfield[75].

In ICA's application, the page is turned on its side to landscape layout in order to create a horizontal outline or a 'chart' of the material being studied. Usually the chapters of a nonfiction book are numbered. In an essay the reader numbers each paragraph in sequence. A horizontal line is drawn a third of the way down the paper and divided into the number of paragraphs in the essay or the chapters of a book. This immediately creates a graphic that allows one to see the whole of the essay in one image.

The key words and ideas in each paragraph are written under the line. (In the example above, the subtitles of the chapter are used as the detail in the sections rather than key words from paragraphs.) The reader quickly skims the content to get a sense of the whole work. Structural clues such as "in the first place" or "after that," or content clues such as subtitles can also be captured at this stage. The next major step is to find the major sections within the work. Dividing lines are drawn upwards from the horizontal line to denote the shift to new sections. Each section focuses on a distinct topic. The sections are titled to reflect the major focus or point. Often sections can be combined into larger topics, because a long essay might consist of several major topics, and each major topic of several subtopics. This structure provides the reader or group with a unified image of the major points the author is making in the work. Finally, the whole work is given a title that summarizes what the

---

74 Adler and Van Doren, 1972
75 Stanfield, 2012

Four-level Chart

Paper: Boulding, THE IMAGE

Behaviour, Images, Messages - Role of values in image change: Theory of Knowledge

Topical

Images Determine Behaviour

Arenas of Knowing (Practical Behaviour)					Img Dets
Space	Time	Rels	Nat	Emot	Beh.
1	2	3	4	5	6
1	2	3	4	5	key

How Impact of Messages Affects Images

Message Affects Img		No ch add	Revolutionary Change			Qualitative Change		
rais-es?	stmt							
7	8	9	10	11	12	13	14	15
		1 & 2		3			4	

Images in Relation to Values and Facts

Dynamic of Value in Image Change:

Image and Value		Value resist	Stabil-ity		No Facts		Soc. Cons.	
stmt	ext.	push		clarific.	an ex	facts	U.D.	med
16	17	18	19	20	21	22	23	24
introduct.			1	2	sol!	?	-	-
					shock		clarificat.	

Issue of Objective Fact

Theory of Knowledge

Rel. to Past		Organic Theory	
epist.	grwth	grwth	behv
25	26	26	27
rel. to past	1	1	2
what it is			

Functional

List of examples — introduces the subject (setting the scene) 1st prop.

con — intro. — clarifies the subject (on stage) 2nd prop. — discussion

key thesis — depth discussion (the major address of paper) key prop.

implications — summary - imp (curtain call) — what it is

Propositional

Human behaviour is determined by images.

The meaning of a message is the impact it makes on images: no or little change, revolutionary change, or qualitative change.

Value, which is present in every image, explains its resistance to change; the process of change, and its relative stability.

All "facts" are formed from images filtered through a changeable value system.

All so-called facts are from a perspective of value: objectivity is at root a social convention.

All this points to a shift in our theory of knowledge to explain practical behaviour.

This paper of THE IMAGE is about a new theory of knowledge that emphasizes behaviour, the impact of messages, and how value is a key function of understanding knowledge change.

Imaginal

Image/picture

What happened to me — My naive grasp of objectivity was exploded.

My response - imperative - decisions — I need to look at the value screen I'm presently using.

Critique — This paper needs more thinking through in Section IV.

FIGURE 24

Sample four-level chart of the introductory concepts in Chapter 1 of a book

CHAPTER 7. SOCIAL PIONEER									
Deciding to respond in a new way			Images of the mission of the social pioneer				The action of the social pioneer		Leadership challenges
Do I dare?	Living on behalf of the future	Creating new models and systems	The mission of the social pioneer	Between the no longer and not yet	Addressing major social concerns	Qualities of the social pioneer	The task of the social pioneer	How can I get started?	

FIGURE 25

A topical chart of the content of a chapter of a book

author is saying. This has been referred to as a "topical" chart. As Gealy[76] says, speaking of reading the New Testament of the *Bible*, "Integrity demands that we attempt to discover, impartially, what Matthew, Mark, Paul, John and Luke have to say – to allow them to speak for themselves." The *Bhagavad Gita*, the *Torah*, a novel by James Joyce, or a complex policy document can be viewed in the same way.

The same work can also be charted functionally. Clarifying the role and function of each part in the whole helps in understanding the structure of the writer's thought. This process facilitates a deeper understanding of way the author puts together their ideas, and helps clarify questions. It is a very useful tool for literary criticism, policy analysis and academic interpretation.

Similarly, following Adler and Van Doren's approach, one can create a *propositional chart*. The reader works through the sections and states the author's points in their own words. Finally, one can create what has been called an *existential chart* that describes the impact of each part of the work and the whole work on their own life. These approaches have been called levels in the charting process, as each level reveals more to us.

The Phenomenology behind the charting method

Intentional focus

Often when we read something, we begin to argue or raise questions with the text before we have even absorbed its message. When we do this, we miss valuable insight and can stay stuck in our previous understandings. We may not even know what we are disagreeing with if we have not listened carefully. This collapses a dialogue into a monologue where we only listen to ourselves. The intentional focus of the charting method is to deeply understand what an author is saying, in order to allow honest dialogue between the author and the reader.

---

76 Gealy, circa 1960s

Radical openness

Charting enables a reader to stay open by setting aside or 'bracketing' all previous understandings, suspending our assumptions, and preparing to listen. One looks at what is actually being said to enable the writer to reveal new insight and make an impact on the reader. Only then, after understanding what the author is actually saying, one is prepared to relate to the work contextually and existentially. The reader allows their being to be altered in the encounter with another and names the impact of the ideas and the choices they believe they must make.

Method of inquiry

The method of inquiry in the charting method follows four basic stages, creating a visual image for each. The reader moves incrementally through levels of understanding, and articulating a relationship to the message of the paper.

Level 1. Topical understanding

The topics give impressions of the broad inclusive images of content. They provide simple answers to the question: What is this section about?

Level 2. Functional understanding

The functions clarify the structural relationship of all the sections of your chart: (introduction, conclusion, thesis or main points, transition, and so on). These terms are simple answers to the question: What role does this section play in the paper?

Level 3. Propositional understanding

Propositions state what is in each paragraph or each section of the structure of the paper, and finally the whole paper. The propositions organize the interior content of each paragraph and section. This is still stating what the author means, articulated in your own words.

Level 4. Existential understanding

This level has to do with how the paper's message affects you personally. This level is never absent; it is about engagement with the paper, but it is at this stage where it finally becomes prominent.

Figure 24 shows a four-level chart of the first 27 paragraphs of Chapter 1 of *The Image: Knowledge in Life and Society*, by Kenneth Boulding.[77]

Design patterns

The basic design pattern follows a set of charting procedures that are similar to the four levels of the focused conversation method. You are structuring your own conversation with the author.

---

77 Boulding, 1956

Part 1. Getting started

Getting a grasp of the whole paper or book

As a phenomenological process, the initial steps move incrementally through the process of really being aware of the author's content. This first stage is quite rapid.

1. Decide to love the paper or book—feel it, pronounce the author's name, look at the covers, etc.
2. Explore the entire contents—take a quick look at subtitles, opening and closing paragraphs, words that jump out at you, and guess what the whole paper or book is about.
3. Number the paragraphs in the paper, the chapters if it is a book, or the sentences if you are charting a particularly convoluted paragraph.
4. Lay out the chart in landscape orientation. Place your paper with the long side across and draw a horizontal line, perhaps a third of the way down, across the length of the paper (sometimes 8 ½" x 14" or A1 paper helps). Divide the line into as many sections as there are paragraphs (or chapters), and number the spaces to correspond with the numbering in the document. Do this very quickly. This is a working chart, not a final copy.
5. Quickly scan for structure—don't read, but look quickly for transitional clues, numerals, italics, transitional words. Highlighting or underlying structural clues can be really helpful. Read, at most, the first four words of each paragraph or chapter. Record findings on work chart below the line. *(Functional clues)*
6. Quickly scan for content. Again, don't read. Look for simple topical headings, and read, at most, the first and last sentence of each paragraph or chapter, scribbling what you find below the line. Don't necessarily start with the first paragraph, but start where topics emerge easily. Then complete all the paragraphs. *(Topical clues)*

Part 2. The depth dialogue

How to ask the paper good questions and hear answers

At this point you begin to articulate your personal response, with impressions and questions that still allow the author to have their say, while at the same time beginning a dialogue with the author.

1. What are the sections emerging in your chart? Draw lines up from the baseline to separate the sections. What functions does each section play (introduction, conclusion, transition, etc.)? Give each section an impressionistic title. Record it above the line. *(Functional level)*
2. You still have not read the paper. Where do you need more data?
   Ask your questions, read in appropriate places, and record your findings below the line in the sections. *(Topical level)*
3. What questions are you now raising about a) the structure of the paper, and b) the content of the paper? Read to complete your picture of the paper and answer your questions. Don't read just to be reading. Keep your side of the dialogue engaged. *(Topical level leading to propositional level)*
4. Organize your findings into a total picture above the line. Give each of the important paragraphs a title that holds the author's meaning in your own words. Give each section a

meaningful title in a consistent way, such as with similar parts of speech. Give a good title to the whole paper that holds the author's meaning in your own words. *(Propositional level)*

5. Ascertain where the key questions and paragraphs of the paper are. Mark or record these on your chart for further exploration into the heart of the paper.

6. In a mirror image of the structure extended below the line, write a brief proposition in your own words stating what is in each paragraph or each section of your structure, and finally the whole paper. The propositions organize the interior content of each paragraph and section. *(Propositional level)*

7. Finally, either at the bottom of the page or on the back of the holding chart, answer these four questions: *(Existential level)*

    a. What shifts in your understanding or images of the topic has this paper provoked for you?

    b. What does this call into question in your current life?

    c. What positive contribution has this paper made to your self-understanding?

    d. What is your critical appraisal of this paper?

Design pattern variations: other types of charts

Teaching chart

When teaching a seminar, the leader can present a teaching chart made ahead of time to help summarize complex content. It includes key points, good questions, images, illustrations, the amount of time to spend on each section, etc.

Art chart

This simplified chart helps communicate the drama of the paper. Added graphics can help focus on the meaning.

Reverse charting

Charting can also be used in reverse to determine the structure of a paper, report, or book, especially in team writing. In this process, the authors brainstorm the content of the paper, perhaps using the consensus workshop method to cluster the individual ideas into areas of similar content. Then the content can be structured into a chart to create the flow of the ideas in the paper. The horizontal format gives a different picture of the content than an outline. It helps you see the flow and how the content builds to a conclusion.

Impact of the charting method

Like many students, when I graduated from university I owned a large number of textbooks that I found very interesting and useful, and did not want to get rid of. But after several moves where I had to lug heavy boxes of books from one place to the next, I decided something had to happen. I took each textbook in turn, and charted their content. I made sure to include all the seminal points that I found useful, adding extra pages when necessary. I put all the charts in one binder, and suddenly my entire collection was not only easy to carry with me, but easily available when I needed the knowledge.

A Catholic education client asked for a course to train school leaders, with a section on how canonical law affected the ways schools made decisions. Someone copied, cut and pasted together a document that included a wide variety of excerpts from canonical law that affect education. A cursory reading could not discover any reason for the way they had put it together. So the facilitator charted the document, and discovered a logical flow to the document that made the whole piece make sense. When the teaching chart was presented, the participants were able to understand that section and teach it to others.

One large organization had only 90 minutes to understand the implications of a long and complicated new policy, so that they could plan how to change their actions to comply with the policy. The facilitators prepared for the meeting by charting the document, and posting a large visual chart on the wall. The group was divided into small groups. Each small group skimmed and then summarized the key points of a section. (This is sometimes called the jigsaw method.) They posted their summaries on the wall under the visual chart of their section and reported back to the group. There were some questions of clarification of each group, and then they discussed the results. After the 90 minutes everyone in the group understood the implications of the policy for their work. The facilitation then continued as the group planned their response.

A team consisting of representatives from a major utility and a First Nation had been working together for several years to resolve a major 40-year-old conflict. They were tasked with writing a report about the situation, what they had learned from their work, and their conclusions. The group first used the consensus workshop method to brainstorm all the things they needed to include in the report. There were 10 clusters of points, each cluster a major topic. The group decided that each cluster was a separate chapter. They arranged the titles of the clusters in the form of a chart, with an executive summary, introduction, core content chapters, and a conclusion. Then, using the chart and the brainstormed data under each column, they sat down in pairs that included one person from each side of the conflict, and wrote prose that communicated the brainstormed content. These draft chapters were edited by other teams, and a 60-page report was written in a matter of days. The conflict was eventually resolved, with the clear supporting documentation from the report.

Conclusion

The charting method is an extraordinary study method that uses visual tools to effectively understand and record the core insights of an author and their relationships within the document, while fostering authentic dialogue between the reader and the author.

12.
ToP Seminar Methodology

Education either functions as an instrument which is used to facilitate integration of the younger generation into the logic of the present system and bring about conformity or it becomes the practice of freedom, the means by which men and women deal critically and creatively with reality and discover how to participate in the transformation of their world.

—Paolo Friere[78]

Too often in study you have learned to hate, rather than love, and when you hate you do not really study or learn…. I will never forgive some of my professors who taught me to listen to what was wrong…. When I was looking for something that was wrong, I could not study because I could not change, for I had all the answers before I looked at that document.

—Joseph Mathews[79]

In an advanced facilitation training course, we use the seminar methodology to train facilitators, using a paper called "Facilitation from the Inside Out" by John Epps[80]. After creating a chart of the paper together (as in Chapter 11), we break people up into small groups to find the key points and visual images of each section, which they post on the wall chart. Then we have a conversation about the paper, which asks participants for examples of where they have experienced the key points in their own lives. Finally, we ask them to reflect on what the paper is saying to them about profound or transformational facilitation, and what impact the paper has on them—the "so what" of studying the paper.

The combination of demythologizing, grounding abstraction or story in real life (see Chapter 2, page 16), with charting evolved into what has been called the seminar method. Its primary

---

78 Friere
79 Matthews, 1968
80 Epps, 2005

application is in the group study of books and essays with the intent of integrating the insights of the study into their life choices.

Background

Briefly, the seminar method involves several steps.
1. A seminar begins with the object of study, such as an essay or a chapter from a book.
2. The group creates a topical chart to summarize what the author says.
3. Individuals express their intuitive impressions and reflective responses, including real-life examples from their experience.
4. Together the group explores the context and engages in interpretative dialogue.
5. Individuals, and sometimes the group as a whole, determine the significance of the study for their own lives, and clarify their decisions and commitments in relation to the topic.

Application

The seminar method is used for participatory education rather than facilitation. In a seminar, the group is not asked to create its own solutions or make its own decisions (as in facilitation), but to learn from an author. Usually the decisions coming out of this kind of seminar are personal decisions about how to relate to the content of the author (education). The seminar starts with the charting method described in Chapter 11 (p 148-155) and continues with group dialogue with the material being studied.

This kind of seminar goes beyond intellectual understanding and argument. It is designed to encourage participants to struggle with deep questions that the author raises about their assumptions and images of themselves and the world.

The phenomenology behind the seminar method

Intentional focus

The *intentional focus* of the seminar method is on the dialogue between the ideas of an author of a paper and the participants in a group studying that paper. The ideas of the author are deeply respected, as the group takes the ideas and explores their significance in their own lives. Participants make choices about how to relate to the author's ideas, but only after deeply exploring their relevance in their own lives.

Radical openness

The *radical openness* of this process is the discipline to take time for the group to thoroughly understand the content of the author's message first, before allowing people to react to the content. The process is also open to the struggle of the participants, who may or may not respond positively to what the author says. The leader can ask tough questions that cause people to examine their reactions, and become more open to others' responses as well.

PREPARING TO TEACH A SEMINAR

Place:	Paper to be studied				Date:
Put your chart of the paper here					
What point in the paper do you want everyone to understand? (Rational Aim)	What do you want to happen to the group? (Existential Aim)	What kind of people are in the group?	What is the mood of the seminar to be? What style will enable that?	When should the high point be? (Overall Drama)	

Title of the Seminar:

Prelude	1. Introducing the subject: paragraphs #s	2. Experimental digging into the subject: paragraph #s	3. Depth dealing with the heart of the matter: paragraph #s	Postlude
		For each of these sections, create questions that will allow the group to answer:		
What will you say first?	What is the author saying? 1. 2. 3. 4.	How is this true of life as I experience it? 1. 2. 3. 4.	What does this say about my life? 1. 2. 3. 4.	To close, what is the provocative question or statement you will leave the group with?
What will you use to get the group's attention to open?				What will you say last?
What hook will you use to motivate the group?				How will you get offstage?
(Overall Introduction)	(Development)	(Climax)	(Resolution)	(Dénouement)
Board Images or Stories				
Time				

FIGURE 26

Template that includes all the steps to prepare to lead a seminar

Method of inquiry

The method of inquiry starts with carefully understanding an author's message. Usually the charting method is used first individually, and then with the group, because it has several levels of understanding built into the process. (See Chapter 11 on page 152.) The group discussion is then focused on grounding the author's key points in real life experience, and pulling meaning out of the dialogue between the author and the participants. The seminar finishes with integration of what individuals or the group have learned from the dialogue into their own lives.

Design patterns

The facilitative educator prepares thoroughly for a seminar, making their own chart and thinking through the key points that the group needs to wrestle with. Then the facilitator decides what the rational and experiential aims of the session will be, and plans the specific steps of the seminar, making sure that there is adequate time spent on the key points. Figure 26 offers a template for preparing a seminar.

The charting step begins the seminar with each person creating a chart of the essay. Each individual does their own work and works through the material on their own, frequently before the meeting. The facilitator then works with the whole group, building on the individual charts, to create a common topical chart that serves as a point of reference for the rest of the seminar. In this step, individuals share the key words and ideas, how they divided the content into sections, and their titles for the various parts of the paper. When different people's titles differ, the facilitator directs the group back to the author's own words. The group can quickly grasp and summarize the basic content of the article as the author meant it, so the author can "have their say." The facilitator keeps the group focused on "the thing itself" for this part of the seminar.

Sometimes, if time is limited, instead of having the participants make their own charts, the facilitator creates a teaching chart ahead of time, and displays it where the whole group can see it, either projected or written on a large wall chart. This chart provides the concrete focus for the group work.

After the chart is done so there's a visual picture of the whole, group discussion begins and progresses section by section through the article. The facilitator guides the *reflective* conversation, enabling the participants to explore initial impressions, associations and responses. When people are clear about what the author is saying and they become conscious of their response, the discussion moves to interpretation.

In the *interpretive* stage, people explore the context and express insight into the meaning, significance and implications of the article's message in relation to their own existential questions. They engage in contextual interpretation. If the group has a common sense of identity and purpose, they will likely discuss an article as it impacts them and their work together as well as how it impacts individual people. A group of random individuals, such as a class, will likely focus on the meaning for them individually. The final step involves questions that enable each individual to determine the impact of the ideas on their own lives and make their own decisions in relation to it. This can be very profound, as each person grapples with their relationship to life through the article.

The primary leadership role is that of guide who encourages deep dialogue. It is a distinct approach to teaching in that it is highly participatory and that the teacher adopts methods of engaging the students in self-examination and dialogue that lead to insight and its application in one's life.

The uniqueness of the seminar methodology is that it is deeply appreciative. Its major intent is to understand the wisdom of the author first as expressed in the book or paper, and only then to explore and ground the impact that wisdom has on the participants. It is not about debating the topic, or critiquing how the author expressed their ideas. Participants leave pondering the significance of new insights to their own lives.

Applications

Usually, the seminar method is not used as a facilitation tool, because it is about wrestling with personal learning, not about creating a shared consensus.

However, a group may need to explore an abstract concept in depth together, in order to ground the abstraction in reality and have the deep conversation they need.

And a seminar can be used to teach facilitators, as in the opening story of this chapter. In the study of the paper "Facilitation from the Inside Out"[81], facilitators are exposed to the idea that facilitation is about more than "masking tape," or simple activities and just getting a group to a product. John Epps proposes in his paper that facilitation is also about *guiding* the group in a number of profound ways. Participants in the study struggle with the roles that he proposes, which give them a way to consciously choose the facilitator role they want to play.

In *The Courage to Lead*[82] study sessions offered by ICA Canada, each session is seen in the context of a leadership compass, which is an overall contextual guide through which to view aspects of leadership. You could see the compass as a diagrammatic image or chart of the book as a whole. The orientation session starts off strong with a dramatic story and shares the reflection process, which is rooted in the focused conversation method.

Before participants come to each study session, they read a chapter and review its chart it in their study guide with key questions. After this initial dialogue with the author, their time in the study session is focused on whole group work with the main concepts, and small group exercises that ground the key points in their lives. They share stories and wrestle with how they experience the dynamics of leadership highlighted in that chapter. The integration (decisional) level focuses on what difference this leadership dynamic makes for them. The last session of the course works through specific challenges people are facing in their workplace or lives, applying the insights from each chapter in the compass. This program has had a strong impact on participants, such as people

---

81 Epps, *ibid*
82 Stanfield, 2012, p 1

with all kinds of jobs in the University Health Network of hospitals. And through the process, people learn to reflect and see the impact of applying their reflections to their daily life. They see how to lead in their unique situations. As the former Senior Development Manager in Human Resources put it, "Everyone can lead from where they stand."

Conclusion

The seminar method is a valuable tool for catalyzing thoughtful responses to provocative materials. It can enable deep learning from participants, while respecting the ideas and work of an author.

13.
ToP Foundations Conclusion

Three simple ideas—description, phenomenon, intentionality—provided enough inspiration to keep roomfuls of Husserlian assistants busy in Freiburg for decades. With all of human existence awaiting their attention, how could they ever run out of things to do?

—Sarah Bakewell[83]

Existentialism

It should very clear by now that existentialist thought played a major role in shaping the foundations of ToP. Existentialism is a vast and highly complex approach to living and to fully describe it would be a project of its own. To engage in an oversimplification, two major strands of existentialist thought and practice have been woven together to form the foundations of ToP methodology. One flowed through Husserl, Heidegger and Sartre who were 'non-theists' in that they did their work outside the context of religious faith. They were philosophers and along with their existentialistic approaches, they were the phenomenologists who began developing processes of inquiry, understanding, forming conclusions and making choices. The other strand is made up of Christian theologians, including Rudolph Bultman, Paul Tillich, Dietrich Bonheoffer and H. Richard and Reinhold Neibuhr, who adopted an existential approach to the practice of their faith. They looked to the more secular phenomenologists for a method that would enable them to demythologize and derive existential meaning from scripture. They applied the insights of the phenomenologists in developing a methodology for the process they called 'demythologizing' sacred literature.

Colleagues of the Institute of Cultural Affairs were deep in the heart of that movement. It provided the heart and soul of work for years to come. True to the spirit and practice of demythologizing was the understanding that each person had to do it for themselves, in their own most specific context, in their own tradition. As a result, academics and clergy were engaging in a new form of

---

83 Bakewell, 2016, p 46

dialogue. As such movements do, it began with a very small core and expanded through much of the Christian community in North America and Europe. They dove into an inquiry that resulted in an entirely new way of understanding and practicing one's most foundational understanding of what it means to be human. They took the advice of the phenomenologists and developed not only a cohesive 20th century theology, but they refined the phenomenological approach itself.

This is an immense body of knowledge and we an only provide a very brief overview. Our intent was to examine the core ideas without exploring the many and very important nuances in depth. It is, I believe, this core that provides much of the foundation for the practice of ToP methodology. It is the most basic set of assumptions about life that we use as foundations for our values, mental models, and actions.

For many, these understandings are expressed most fully in a faith context, but they are also far beyond that. While the search for foundational understandings was driven from within a specific context, it was done for the sake of how that meaning was expressed in one's lived life in the world regardless of one's faith, external conditions or situation. It was a search for the core characteristics of what it means to be human.

It must be recognized that all of these dynamical elements contribute to our ontological foundation. They form a response to a question Dr. Joep van Arendonk of UNFPA once posed, "What is it to be (hu)man?", in a lecture where he called ICA the "People of the Question".[84] This is, as William Cozart pointed out in his 1966 essay on cybernetics, "to examine ourselves as a species."[85] As Dr. van Arendonk reminded us, we have dedicated our efforts over the years to asking those foundational questions of 'being-human' and 'being-in-the-world-with-purpose'. They arise out of our work and are matured by our application and learning.

We have, over the years, created many models to represent what it is to be human. Each of them has been done from a unique perspective with specific focus and has been done by applying a disciplined approach with integrity. Each has contributed to our understanding and practice. As with all models, this attempt is temporal and will evolve as we explore, experiment, practice and learn.

Building these models and trying to make sense of our situation in the world is a search. What we find in that search are some basic aspects of what it is to be human. It is difficult to isolate them, because they can only be seen as they function in a networked, interactive, dynamical complex. We find our being in their interaction. Isolating them is only creating a mental model. This is what makes modeling it a challenge.

This is one reality, the 'field' of our being. The self is the active being. It is the relating, choice-making self. It is the core and, yet it is only activated in and by our real situation, 'being-in-itself.' Its only content is our real situation. We exist as who we are in the here and now. We are grounded in this set of relationships and in this moment. This is 'being-in-itself', our real situation.

84 Van Arendonk, 1986
85 Cozart, William, 1966

We exist as ontologically free beings acting in profound responsibility. That is 'being-for-itself', self or spirit.

> *Be strong then, and enter into your own body;*
> *There you have a solid place for your feet.*
> *Think about it carefully!*
> *Don't go off somewhere else?*
> *Kabir says this: just throw away all thoughts of imaginary things,*
> *And stand firm in that which you are.*[86]

The Future of ToP

ToP Methods can be effective for beginners as well as those who've finely honed their expertise. Whatever their experience, the integrity of the method and the philosophy behind it extend the capacity of both the facilitator and a group.

For a beginner, simply using the structure of the Focused Conversation method or the Consensus Workshop method to design and facilitate group work will increase a group's capacity to process information and reach thoughtful conclusions.

For an experienced practitioner, the underlying structure and disciplined thought processes inherent in the ToP methods make it possible to adapt them effectively for new contexts.

For a very experienced facilitator wanting to help individuals and groups transform themselves and their situations ToP methods can be used consciously to unblock inhibiting underlying images and release the potential of a group.

As stated in the introduction, ToP methods aim to build off the deep undercurrents of history, deal with some major contradictions of our day, create a new paradigm of participation, and bring about profound transformations in people and society.

These methods are designed to work with the way human beings think clearly, when they think clearly. The key to this is the underlying phenomenological method.

The methods can and have been used formally and informally over the past 50 years in almost every culture, sector of society, and kind of group in the world; from village meetings to corporate executive teams; in Nigeria, Russia, China, Korea, Peru, Australia; with preschool-age children to elders; with non-profits, governments, businesses and schools.

Some keys to applying ToP methods well include
- Respecting that the group has wisdom and can create its own solutions or results
- Being conscious of one's own preferences and biases, and setting those aside while facilitating the group in order to hear what the group is saying
- Taking time to understand the underlying dynamics of the methods

---

86 Bly, 1993

- Carefully designing an overall process to take advantage of how each particular method addresses the need of the group and its journey
- Taking time to reflect with the group on their experience

As we continue to use and develop these methods globally, we are challenged to adapt the processes to emerging technologies and cultural preferences, and incorporate new ideas while maintaining alignment with the core phenomenology of the methods. Continuing dialogue between practitioners to share insights and learnings, as well as to question each other's assumptions, will be necessary to sustain the deeper possibilities of the methods.

A continuing challenge at this time is how to most effectively use the methods with online platforms and social media, maximizing participation, insight and innovative results.

Since these are human methods, it is safe to say that they will continue to evolve while retaining the phenomenological essence that makes them work.

Conclusion

We must return to the beginning. It can be said that the objective and reflective levels of ToP methods play the primary role in enabling us to "relate ourselves to ourselves", as Kierkegaard put it, and the interpretive and decisional levels primarily enable us to will ourselves to be ourselves.

As we "experience our experience", we articulate our perception of what actually happened or what we see as well as our initial responses, reactions, associations, memories, feelings and intuitions. When we name them, they become part of our conscious world. We are no longer trapped in simply saying, "It happened, it happened, it happened." We begin to relate ourselves to ourselves and become more aware of who we are in a situation–more self-conscious and able to move on.

We are not stuck in a world of pre-rational feeling about ourselves in our situation. We can begin to identify what is of substance and meaning for us. We, in the end, make choices. Inasmuch as those choices are made with authenticity and integrity, we will ourselves to be ourselves by integrating our insight into our real lives.

As we move through each level, the information surfaced becomes the foundation for the next steps. It becomes the '*en-soi*' or 'being-in-itself', as Sartre called it. Objectifying the basic information brings it into awareness. Reflecting on that basic information brings our responses to full consciousness and our reflection becomes the ground we stand upon to enter into interpretation. Our insight, then, becomes the platform upon which we make decisions and articulate transcendent significance. In the end, we have a new situation–an entirely new being-in-itself. We recreate ourselves at every turn.

—Wayne Nelson

Appendix

Wisdom is like a pocket watch.
Only take it out when you need it.

—E. M. Mings

Working Assumptions

1. Everyone has wisdom.

2. We need everyone's wisdom for the wisest result.

3. There are no wrong answers.

4. The whole is greater than the sum of its parts.

5. Everyone will be heard and will hear others.

©Canadian Institute of Cultural Affairs, 1996, 2000

Figure 27
Working assumptions poster

Explanation of each working assumption

1. **Everyone has wisdom.** (This doesn't mean that everything that everyone says is wise. It means that behind what they say is wisdom, and we will listen for it.)
2. **We need everyone's wisdom for the wisest result.** (In the same way that a diamond is more valuable when it is cut with more facets, what we come up with will be more valuable when we have illuminated more facets of what we are working with.)
3. **There are no wrong answers.** (See assumption 1. Behind what may seem on the surface as a wrong answer—and I have heard some that were positively evil on the surface—there is wisdom, and that is what we will listen for. The corollary, of course, is that there are no right answers, only the best we can come up with given our limitations.)
4. **The whole is greater than the sum of its parts.** (Trite, yes, but this assumption points to consensus as creating a larger answer that is not identical to any one view, but includes the wisdom of many. Again, consider the diamond. I think of compromise as smaller than the sum of its parts, consensus as larger. It's like a puzzle picture, which is the sum of the puzzle pieces and their relationships. All puzzle pieces are included, or there is a hole in the result.)
5. **Everyone will hear others and be heard.** (This doesn't mean that everyone has to talk all the time—then nobody would be heard! It means listening to others as well as making sure your wisdom is on the table.)

<table>
<tr><td colspan="6">Topic</td></tr>
<tr><td rowspan="2">Opening</td><td colspan="2">Rational Aim(s)</td><td colspan="2">Experiential Aim(s)</td><td rowspan="2">Closing</td></tr>
<tr><td>Objective</td><td>Reflective</td><td>Interpretive</td><td>Decisional</td></tr>
</table>

Figure 28

Focused conversation method worksheet

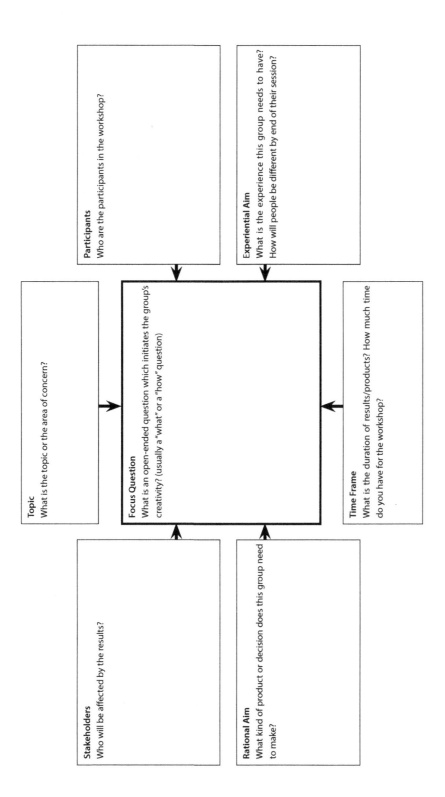

Figure 29

Focus question worksheet for a consensus workshop

Topic				
Context	Rational Aim(s)		Experiential Aim(s)	Resolve
	Brainstorm	Cluster	Name	

Figure 30
Consensus workshop method worksheet

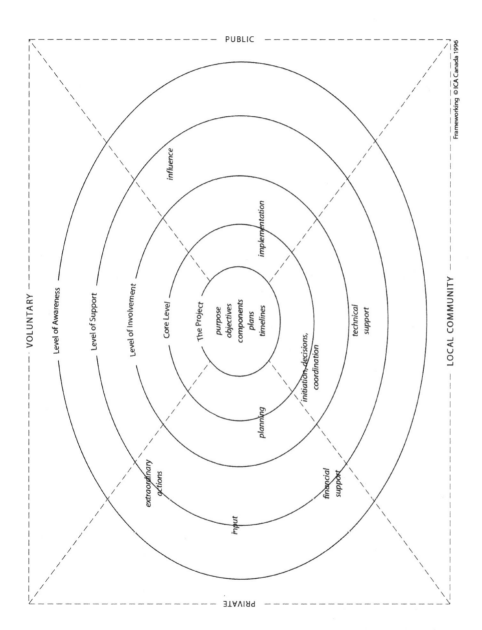

Figure 31

Frameworking worksheet used to analyze the framework of involvement and support around a project. It can be used to determine who is currently involved with a project at which level, who needs to be involved, and to create strategies to involve them at an appropriate level.

Guided daydreaming script for visioning exercise
"Guided daydreaming" script to help a group create a vision

Priming the pump: enabling the vision brainstorm to be comprehensive

I often use the social process triangles (see page 187) as a way to ensure comprehensive thinking in the brainstorm, especially for vision workshops. If the focus question is very different, I adapt this approach considerably, using as comprehensive a screen as I can dream up. I find I adapt this very intuitively, in response to the group.

Vision visualization

I usually call it *daydreaming* to clients.

Preparation: prepare the page for a mind-map.

First, ask them to turn a piece of blank paper sideways and write the focus question in the middle of the page, then draw a circle around it; you can demonstrate this on a flip chart. I tell them that I don't think in outline form—my mind "sproings" from one idea to another. I ask who else is like that (usually almost everybody). Explain that mindmapping is one way of holding ideas as they come, and allowing relationships to grow. Show on the flipchart that the focus question is like the trunk of a tree and that ideas branch out from each other— you draw a separate branch for each idea and hold it in a few words or a visual image. Eventually you may connect different branches with lines as well. Give participants permission to use this way of writing their ideas if it is comfortable, or to use any other way they like to record their ideas.

Then ask them to put their pencils down.

"Who in this room likes to daydream? I'm going to give you a chance to daydream this afternoon. Some people like to look out the window, others to look at the ceiling, others to close their eyes—some rest their head on their hands so the boss thinks they're working hard . . . . You may relax a little bit and get into a comfortable position for daydreaming—but not too comfortable so that you fall asleep!"

Allow your voice to become soft and relaxed, and slow the pace down. It helps to look at the ceiling and also imagine as you talk so that the pace and the ambiance work for everyone. (This sample script uses the focus question "What do we want to see in our community in the next five years?")

"Imagine for a moment that you are at home in your favourite comfortable chair. You look up at the wall and see a calendar, and you note with surprise that it says (the date five years from today) and you realize that it has been exactly five years since we did the visioning workshop.

You begin to remember all the changes that have happened since the planning, things that you have wanted to come into being in this community. And as you begin to remember, you decide you would like to go out and take a look around the community. You get up and put on your coat, and you notice that on the lapel of your coat is a button that says the name of your organization.

You go out and begin to go around the community, and as you go you begin to notice physical things—buildings and open spaces, and you note the changes that have happened in the last five years, since this year (2017); changes that you have wanted to come into being. You go on a little further, and you notice places where people are working, and the changes that have happened in workplaces and in how people work together in the last five years, since (2017); changes that you have wanted to come into being. You note these things.

You go on a bit further, and you note places where decisions are getting made in the community now in (2022), and where justice is being carried out. You note the changes that have happened in the last five years, since (2017); changes that you have wanted to come into being.

You go on a bit further, and you note places and ways that people are learning now in (2022), changes that you have wanted to come into being. And you note the groups are organized, and perhaps families. And you note how people are symbolizing meaning in their lives now in (2022), And you note all these things.

As you go, someone comes up to you, notices your button, and begins to tell you the changes they've noticed that your organization has made in the community that they've wanted to see. You listen to them and note what they have to say. You say goodbye to them, and a little while later you meet someone else, someone with very different ideas than yours, maybe even opposing ideas, and they begin to tell you the changes that they see that they've wanted to come into being. You note what they have to say as well.

You decide to go to the office, and you note what's on the bulletin board that tells you what's going on now in (2022), Perhaps someone in the office comes up to you and tells you their hopes and dreams and how they have come into being now in (2022),

By this time your mind is very full of all the things that are in place now in (2022), so you decide it's time to go home. You go home, take off your coat, and sit down in your favourite chair, and remember all of the things you have seen and heard that have come into being in the community in (2022) , things that you have wanted to see.

When you are ready, you can come back through time and space into this room and this time, and let your ideas flow from your mind, through your arm and pencil, onto the paper.

(after a little time) There are no wrong answers. Any other things that come to you as you are writing, you may write as well."

Obstacles conversation for use when a consensus workshop is not possible

Now, do you note this little niggle in the back of your mind, "Yeah, but . . . ."? Well, that leads us to the obstacles question. What is blocking our vision?

Everybody take a piece of paper. Write down what comes to mind that answers the question.

Now star your three most important answers.

Everyone listen carefully—go around the circle, each person say one block. (No arguments, only questions of clarity. You can write on a flipchart, but you don't have to.)

Have we left anything out?

Objective: What caught your attention as you heard these?

Reflective: Which of these you heard felt heaviest? Lightest?

Interpretive: Where do you see patterns emerging in these obstacles?

Decisional: (Dandelion image) What are some of the root issues under these? (Write on the flipchart in their words.)

Suggest that they try this grammatical form to state the root issues:

> Block, *how* it blocks, *what* it blocks—such as "Hierarchy stifles creativity"

Decisional: (the focus question for the strategies workshop) What can we do to deal with these root issues and realize our vision? (Use your own strategies focus question here and get at least one answer from each person.)

Task Force Action Planning Workbook

Figures 32-35

The simple or task force action planning workbook

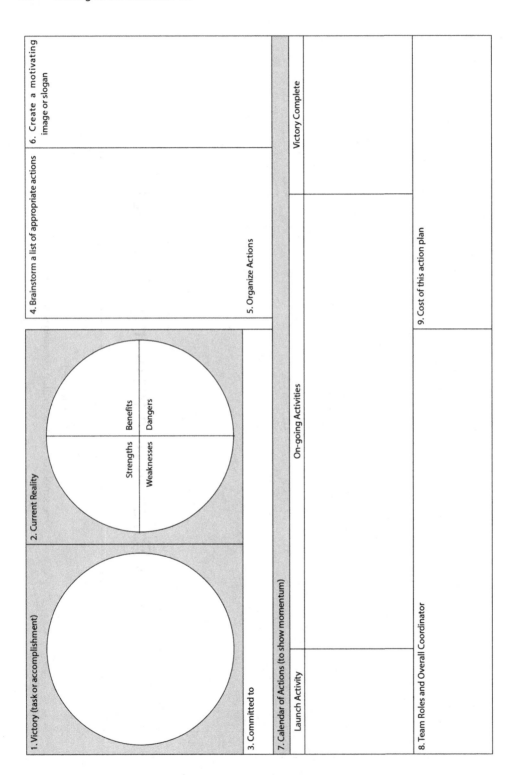

FIGURE 33

Action planning overview

4. Brainstorm a list of appropriate act ons that will accomplish what I have committed to:

6. Create a motivating image or slogan

5. Organize actions: Group the actions into several clusters and/or number them in sequence

FIGURE 34

Brainstore and organize the actions

7. Calendar of Actions (to show momentum)
Plot the actions from Step 5 on the following timeline, including dates you will start the actions where possible

Launch Activity	On-going Activities	Victory Complete

8. Team Roles and Overall Coordinator Who will do these actions? Who will coordinate the activity?	9. Cost of this Action Plan

FIGURE 35

Calendar of actions and assignments

Action Planning Workbook

Figures 36-39

Canadian action planning workbook for use with the strategic planning process

| | | 6. Possible Accomplishments |
| | | Brainstorm possible accomplishments for this time period that build on the advantages and acknowledge the limits. |

1. Strategy
Write in the name of the strategy.

	Advantages	Limits
Present	**2. Strengths** In implementing this strategy at this time, we have the following strengths:	**3. Weaknesses** In implementing this strategy at this time, we have the following weaknesses:
Future	**5. Benefits** in the future of implementing this strategy are:	**4. Dangers** in the future of implementing this strategy are:

7. Measurable Accomplishment
Choose an accomplishment which
• is catalytic
• is realistic
• will have a substantial impact
• will inspire commitment and action.

Taking all the above into consideration, we are committed to the following measurable accomplishment by _____ (date): _

_____
_____

FIGURE 37

Measurable accomplishment worksheet

8. Strategy
Write the name of the strategy on this line.

9. Measurable Accomplishment
Write the measurable accomplishment that you are committed to on this line (from step 7).

10. Specific Actions
List the specific actions needed to complete the measurable accomplishment indicated above.

11. If there are more than ten actions listed in step 10 organize them into clusters that are similar in their action focus. Each cluster should represent a distinct action step.

12. Number the actions in each cluster in the sequence that you will do them.

13. Image/Slogan
Create a motivating image or slogan for this action campaign

FIGURE 38

Worksheet: generate specific actions

14. Strategy	15. Measurable
Write the name of the strategy on this line.	Accomplishment
	Copy from Step 7.

16. Action Timeline
Divide the timeline into the appropriate number of time blocks and write the actions (from Step 12) that you have selected in the appropriate time block on this timeline.

17. Implementing Team
Who will be responsible for implementing this action plan? (at least one person in the planning group; name, not roles)

18. Costs
Write the costs (time and money) of implementing this action plan on lines below:

Money

Time

FIGURE 39

Worksheet: produce action timeline

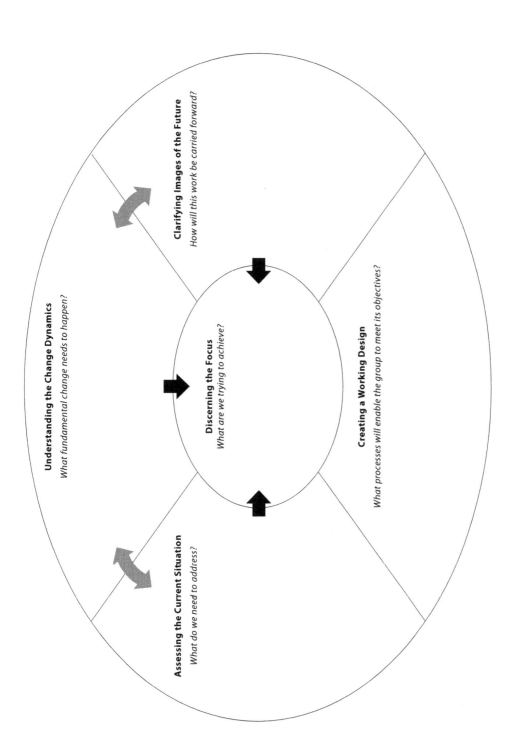

Figure 40
Design Eye worksheet

PREPARING TO TEACH A SEMINAR

Place:	Paper to be studied			Date:
Put your chart of the paper here				
What point in the paper do you want everyone to understand? (Rational Aim)	What do you want to happen to the group? (Existential Aim)	What kind of people are in the group?	What is the mood of the seminar to be? What style will enable that?	When should the high point be? (Overall Drama)

Title of the Seminar:

Prelude	1. Introducing the subject: paragraphs #s	2. Experimental digging into the subject: paragraph #s	3. Depth dealing with the heart of the matter: paragraph #s	Postlude
	For each of these sections, create questions that will allow the group to answer:			
What will you say first?	What is the author saying? 1. 2. 3. 4.	How is this true of life as I experience it? 1. 2. 3. 4.	What does this say about my life? 1. 2. 3. 4.	To close, what is the provocative question or statement you will leave the group with?
What will you use to get the group's attention to open?				What will you say last?
What hook will you use to motivate the group?				How will you get offstage?
(Overall Introduction)	(Development)	(Climax)	(Resolution)	(Dénouement)
Board Images or Stories				
Time				

Figure 41

Seminar planning template

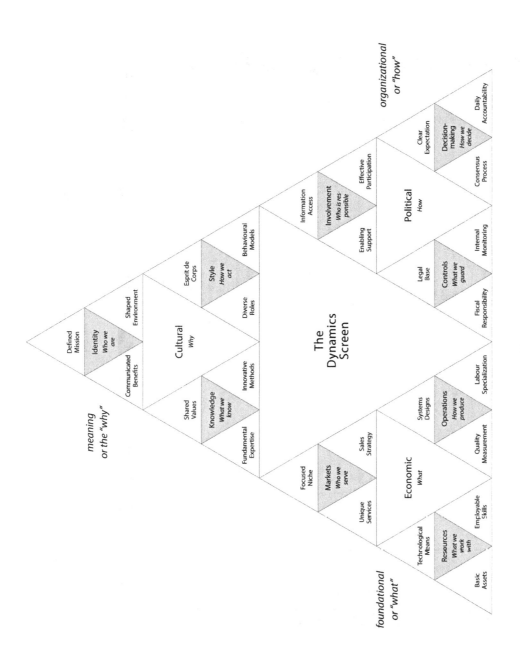

Figure 42

Social process triangles, a comprehensive screen for understanding the social dynamics in any human group

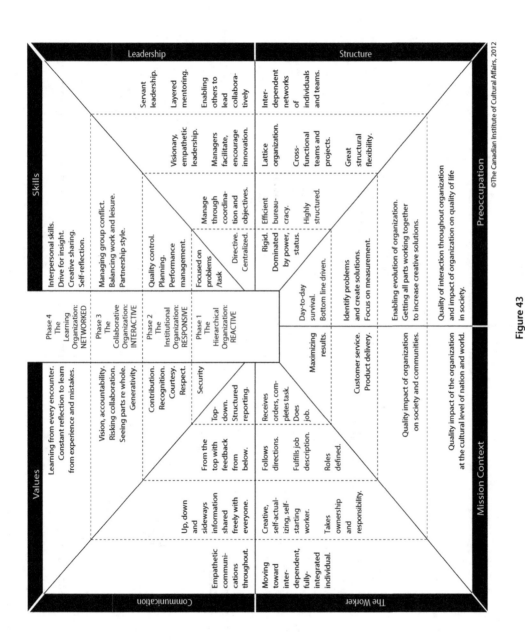

Figure 43

Organizational journey map, a tool for analyzing the culture of an organization, both what it is now and where participants want it to be in the future

Bibliography

Phenomenology and existentialism

Bakewell, Sarah. *At the Existentialist Café: Freedom, Being, and Apricot Cocktails*. New York: Other Press, 2016.

Bultmann, Rudolph. *Essays: Philosophical and Theological*. London: SCM Press, 1955.

Bultmann, Rudolph. "New Testament and Mythology: The Problem of Demythologizing the New Testament Proclamation (1941)." In *New Testament and Mythology and Other Basic Writings*. Philadelphia, PA: Fortress Press, 1941.

Gealy, Fred. "Dialogue and Encounter." In Fred D. Gealy papers, Bridwell Library, Perkins School of Theology, Southern Methodist University. Dallas: TX. circa 1960s.

Heidegger, Martin. *Being and Time*. New York: Harper and Row, 1962.

Heidegger, Martin. *The Origin of the Work of Art*. Waterloo, ON: University of Waterloo, 1963. Accessed through http://www.academia.edu

Husserl, Edmund. *Ideas Pertaining to a Pure Phenomenology and to a Phenomenological Philosophy*. Boston: Kluwer Boston, Inc., 1983.

Husserl, Edmund. *Logical Investigations* (2 volumes). New York: Routledge and Kegan Paul, 1970.

Johnson, Roger A. *Rudolph Bultmann: Interpreting Faith for the Modern Era*. Minneapolis: Fortress Press, 1991.

Kierkegaard, Søren, *Edifying Discourses: A Selection*. New York: Harper, 1958.

Kierkegaard, Søren. *Fear and Trembling and The Sickness Unto Death*. Princeton, NJ: Princeton University Press, 1941.

Kierkegaard, Søren. *Philosophical Fragments*. Princeton: Princeton University Press, 1936.

Merleau-Ponty, Maurice. *Phenomenology of Perception*. New York: Routledge & Kegan Paul, 1962.

Ricoeur, Paul. "Imagination in Discourse and in Action," in *From Text to Action*. Evanston, IL: Northwestern University Press, 1991.

Sartre, Jean-Paul. *Being and Nothingness*. New York: Washington Square Press, 1943.

Scheler, Max. *Selected Philosophical Essays*. Evanston, IL: Northwestern University Press, 1973.

Wertheimer, Max. "An address before the Kant Society." Berlin: 7 December 1924. In the translation by Willis D. Ellis published in his *Source Book of Gestalt Psychology*. New York: Harcourt, Brace and Co., 1938.

Applied phenomenology and methodological theory

Adler, Mortimer and Charles Van Doren. *How to Read a Book*. Toronto: Simon and Schuster, Touchstone, 1972.

Alexander, Christopher. *The Timeless Way of Building*, New York: Oxford University Press, 1979.

Alexander, Christopher, Sara Ishikawa and Murray Silverstein. *A Pattern Language: Towns, Buildings, Construction*. New York: Oxford University Press, 1977.

Baggett, John. *Times of Tragedy and Moments of Grace*. Denver: Outskirts Press, 2009.

Briggs, Robert O. and Gert-Jan de Vreede. *ThinkLets: Building Blocks for Concerted Collaboration*. Lincoln: University of Nebraska Center for Collaboration Science, 2000.

Bohm, David, Donald Factor, and Peter Garret. "Dialogue—A Proposal", transcribed by Richard Burg, 1991. Accessed at http://www.david-bohm.net/dialogue/dialogue_proposal.html

Bohm, David, and F. David Peat. *Science, Order, and Creativity*. New York, Bantam Books, 1987.

Boulding, Kenneth. *The Image: Knowledge in Life and Society*. Ann Arbor: University of Michigan Press, 1956.

Cozart, William. "Cybernetics—Meta Image of the Twentieth Century," in the newsletter of the Ecumenical Institute, Vol. 3, No. 2. November 1966. Accessed at https://top.memberclicks.net/assets/Teams/Virtual_Huddle_Archive/cybernetics%20meta%20image%20of%20the%20twentieth%20century%20.pdf

Dewey, John. *Experience and Education*, New York: Simon & Schuster, Touchstone, 1997.

Dewey, John. *How We Think: A Restatement of the Reflective Thinking to the Educative Process*. Heath, 1933.

Friere, Paolo. *Pedagogy of the Oppressed*. 30th anniversary ed. New York: Bloomsbury Academic, 2000.

Goodstein, Leonard D., Timothy M. Nolan, and J. William Pfeiffer. *Applied Strategic Planning: A Comprehensive Guide*. New York: McGraw Hill, 1993.

International Institute for Facilitation and Change (IIFAC). What Do Facilitators Do, video on YouTube, published April 1, 2013 at https://www.youtube.com/watch?v=UDLGjKBHSXg

Kaner, Sam, "Participatory Decision-Making in Multi-Sectoral Collaboration," presented to the Center for Health Leadership, August 2011. Accessed at http://chl.berkeley.edu/images/stories/conference/kaner.pdf

Kloepfer, John. *The Art of Formative Questioning: A Way to Foster Self-Disclosure*. PhD thesis for Duquesne University, 1990.

Kolb, David. *Experiential Learning: Experience as the Source of Learning and Development*. 2nd ed. Upper Saddle River, NJ: Pearson FT Press, 2015.

Langer, Susanne K. *Philosophy in a New Key: A Study in the Symbolism of Reason, Rite, and Art*. Cambridge: Harvard University Press, 1942.

Langer, Susanne K, *Feeling and Form: A Theory of Art Developed from Philosophy in a New Key*. New York: Scribner, 1953.

Langer, Susanne K, *Problems of Art: Ten Philosophical Lectures*. New York: Scribner, 1957.

McLuhan, Marshall. *Understanding Media: The Extensions of Man*. Cambridge: Massachusetts Institute of Technology Press, 1994.

Mintzberg, Henry. *The Rise and Fall of Strategic Planning*. New York: Simon and Schuster, 1994.

Osborn, Alex. *Applied Imagination*. New York: Scribner, 1953.

Polanyi, Michael. *The Tacit Dimension*. Chicago: University of Chicago Press, 2009.

Rogers, Everett. *A History of Communication Study: A Biological Approach*. New York: The Free Press, 1944.

Scharmer, Otto. *Theory U: Leading from the Future as It Emerges. The Social Technology of Presencing* San Francisco: Berrett-Koehler Publishers, 2009.

Van Arendonk, Dr. Joep. "The People of the Question," speech to the ICA Global Assembly, Bilbao, July 1986. Accessed at https://wedgeblade.net/files/archives_assets/20822.pdf

Van Manen, Max. *Phenomenology of Practice: Meaning-giving Methods in Phenomenological Research and Writing*. New York: Routledge, 2016.

Van Manen, Max, "Phenomenology of Practice." In *Phenomenology & Practice*, I Vol 1, No. 1. 2007, pp. 11-30.

Technology of Participation

Epps, John. "Facilitation from the Inside Out," published in the *IAF Handbook of Group Facilitation*, Ed. Sandy Schuman. San Francisco: Jossey Bass, 2005, pp. 563 – 571.

Jenkins, Jon and Maureen. *The Social Process Triangles*. Groningen, the Netherlands, Imaginal Training, 1997.

Nelson, Jo. *The Art of Focused Conversation for Schools, Over 100 Ways to Guide Clear Thinking and Promote Learning*. 3rd ed. iUniverse, 2013.

Mathews, Joseph W. "Charting." Unpublished lecture delivered in Chicago. November 29, 1968. Accessed through ICA archives https://wedgeblade.net/gold_path/data/meth/100131.htm

Spencer, Laura J. *Winning Through Participation: Meeting the Challenge of Corporate Change with the Technology of Participation*. Dubuque, Iowa: Kendall Hunt, 1989.

Stanfield, R. Brian. *The Art of Focused Conversation: 100 Ways to Access Group Wisdom in the Workplace*. Gabriola Island, B.C.: New Society Publishers, 2000.

Stanfield, R. Brian. *The Courage to Lead: Transform Self, Transform Society*. 2nd ed. The Canadian Institute of Cultural Affairs by iUniverse, 2012.

Stanfield, R. Brian. *The Workshop Book*, Gabriola Island, B.C.: New Society Publishers, 2002.

Stanfield, R. Brian, "The Organizational Journey Map." In *Edges: New Planetary Patterns*, Volume 9 # 2, August 1997.

Staples, Bill. *Transformational Strategy: Facilitation of ToP Participatory Planning*. Bloomington, IN: iUniverse, 2012.

Wilson, Priscilla H., Kathleen Hamish, and Joel Wright. *The Facilitative Way: Leadership That Makes a Difference*. Shawnee Mission, KS: Team Tech Press, 2003.

Williams, R. Bruce. *More than 50 Ways to Build Team Consensus*. Thousand Oaks, CA: Corwin Press, 2000.

Top Training Course Manuals – available through course participation

Group Facilitation Methods: http://www.ica-associates.ca/product/group-facilitation-methods/

US Strategic Planning: ToP Strategic Planning: https://icausa.memberclicks.net/top-strategic-planning

Canadian Strategic Planning: Transformational Strategy: http://www.ica-associates.ca/product/transformational-strategy/

For ToP™ training in other countries, contact your local ICA office http://www.ica-international.org/ica-worldwide

,

Other resources:

Atlee, Tom with Rosa Zubizarreta. *The Tao of Democracy: Using Co-Intelligence to Create a World That Works for All*. North Charleston, SC: Imprint Books, 2003.

Bly, Robert. *The Kabir Book: Forty-Four of the Ecstatic Poems of Kabir*. Boston: Beacon Press, 1993.

Eliot, T.S. *Selected Poems*. London: Faber Modern Classics, 1967.

Kahane, Adam, *Collaborating with the Enemy: How to Work with People You Don't Agree With or Like or Trust*. Oakland, CA: Barrett-Koehler Publishers, Inc., 2017.

Lawrence, D.H. *Selected Poems*. Viking Compass Books, 1959.

Murray, William Hutchison, *The Scottish Himalayan Expedition*. London: Dent and Sons, 1951.

Printed in the United States
By Bookmasters